Reading *with* Meaning

Teaching Comprehension *in the* Primary Grades

Debbie Miller

Foreword by
Ellin Oliver Keene

Stenhouse Publishers
Portland, Maine

Stenhouse Publishers
www.stenhouse.com

Credits
Pages 83, 113, and 114: "Ducks on a Winter Night," "Dressing Like a Snake," and "Song of the Dolphin" from *Creatures of Earth, Sea, and Sky* by Georgia Heard. Copyright © 1992 by Georgia Heard. Published by Wordsong/Boyds Mills Press, Inc. Reprinted by permission.

Library of Congress Cataloging-in-Publication Data
Miller, Debbie, 1948–
Reading with meaning : teaching comprehension in the primary grades / Debbie Miller.
        p. cm.
        Includes bibliographical references and index.
        ISBN 1-57110-307-4 (alk. paper)
        1. Reading (Primary) 2. Reading comprehension. I. Title.
OB1525.7 .M55 2002
372.4—dc21   2002017594

Cover photographs by Debbie Miller and T. John Hughes (center photo)
Cover and interior design by Martha Drury

Manufactured in the United States of America on acid-free paper
10 09 08 07 06 05   20 19 18 17 16 15 14 13 12

To the Public Education and Business Coalition, an organization whose commitment to education inspires us to teach and learn with passion, rigor, and joy

Contents

Work ■ Text-to-Text Connections ■ Schema Throughout the Year ■ Evidence of Understanding and Independence ■ Schema at a Glance

Foreword

There is a mystique about fine primary teachers. There is something transcendent about them—almost superhuman. As a young intermediate teacher, I regarded the fine primary teachers in my building with something like bewildered awe. There was magic in the air down their hallway: those teachers were teaching kids to read, and although I had studied reading theory, I still couldn't figure out how they could do it. What were they doing? What was their secret?

When I approached the primary teachers I most admired and asked them to describe how they taught kids to read, they were often unable to articulate just how all the pieces came together. "I'm not sure," they would say. "I just know what to do. I follow the kids' lead."

When I first met Debbie Miller, my awe grew tenfold. Colleagues had described the warmth of her classroom environment, the depth of her rapport with young children, the seamless way children managed their own behavior in her classroom, her unconditional respect for each child. I couldn't wait to meet another fantastic primary teacher from whom I could learn. But I discovered a profound difference between Debbie and the other fine primary teachers I had known. When I asked Debbie about her beliefs, her approaches, her teaching strategies, she was able to define and describe not just what she did with children, but why.

Debbie began one of our early conversations by sharing a research-based belief statement she had written to guide her practice. She laid out what was working as well as what was puzzling her about the children. She didn't pretend to have the answers, but she knew that through study of children and through professional study, she could explore and eventually articulate exactly why her children learned and responded in the way they did. She was serious about her work in the classroom, but that indescribable magic was there, too.

Debbie was everything my colleagues had described and more. There was, however, one quality they hadn't told me about, and it is one I have come to believe is essential to her success. Debbie was, and is to this day, absolutely fascinated by children. As I came to know her, I realized that she finds nothing so enthralling as kids, and her uncanny ability to describe her successes in the classroom rests on her ardent observation of them.

In *Reading with Meaning* Debbie gives language to the mystique of the superb first-grade literacy teacher. Specifically, she explains the cognitive tools young children need in order to understand. With a written voice so like the one I now know from countless conversations, she describes with humor, respect, awe, curiosity, and joy what it really takes to help children explore and understand their world and the texts written to describe that world.

Debbie articulates like no other teacher I've known what matters most in primary literacy teaching and learning. She makes the indescribable world of young learners clear and real. She also has a novelist's gift for detail. Every reader of this book will laugh and cry and wince and gasp—and, perhaps for the first time, really understand early literacy.

In writing this book, Debbie has undertaken a daunting task: to define and describe the thinking processes a young child uses to understand and what a primary teacher can do to teach those processes. The task is daunting not only because it is difficult to articulate fine practice, but also because all too many people in this country, teachers and nonteachers alike, don't believe that young children are up to the task. Can a first grader, for example, really synthesize as she reads? Come on. Can young children determine importance? If they can, isn't it a fluke? Will they do it again later, with another book? Surely they won't become independent in their use of such strategies. Aren't they really too young to think that abstractly? Don't we really need to focus on comprehension instruction in the upper grades instead?

In *Reading with Meaning* Debbie not only provides conclusive evidence that young children can think strategically when reading, she causes us to rethink every assumption we ever had about what young children can do. She shows how children from widely varying backgrounds and with a huge range of needs can become aware of their own thinking during reading, learn to give language to that thinking, and use it to understand any text more deeply. She shows us how children have an almost infinite ability to understand and discuss even the most abstract ideas.

How does Debbie get her children to think and write and read with the kind of fervor you will read about in this book? She believes they can, she shows them how a proficient reader does it, and she provides the means to make their thinking public. She is focused, purposeful, and clear. But there is another piece, at least as important. As Debbie tells us, there is not enough joy in our classrooms and schools. Given all the public urgency to perform and all the seriousness with which we now approach early literacy learning, there has to be magic, a bit of fun, a lot of joy.

In *Reading with Meaning* Debbie uses the natural seasons of a teaching year to reveal the gradual process of immersing children in a rigorous yet intimate learning environment followed by ways in which she introduces and develops a range of comprehension strategies. As you work your way through the book, you will live through the school year alongside Debbie and her kids, listening in, glimpsing the exquisite development of thought and understanding. By the end of the book, the end of the teaching year, you will see how these first graders have come to understand concepts of extraordinary complexity and how they can use the comprehension strategies independently and with great confidence.

It isn't easy to explain great literacy instruction for young children. So many fine teachers say, "I don't know, it just comes naturally." Debbie shows us that by defining and teaching the cognitive tools we all use to comprehend text, we give children the tools they need to think and understand with unprecedented depth. In this book, which I believe will become a classic in literacy teaching and learning, Debbie Miller defines and describes the instruction, and she tells us about the children's successes. But there is always magic in the mix, a little mystique, a bit of fun, a lot of joy.

Ellin Oliver Keene
January 2002

In Appreciation

We were hot, sticky, and short on patience as we filed into the faculty lounge one afternoon late in May. Lingering smells of pepperoni pizza, microwaved popcorn, and ripe banana mingled with a fresh bouquet of lilacs. We had been summoned by our principal for yet another faculty meeting. "What could it be this time?" we wondered as we sank into the odd assortment of chairs that lined the room.

"Guess what, everybody?" Doris announced cheerily. "We are *all* going to become writers this summer!" Eyes roll. Pencils tap. Tony, the PE teacher, shakes his head and groans. Unfazed, the principal continues. "Raise your hands if you've heard of Shelley Harwayne." Three hands shoot up. "Only three?" she asks, looking shocked and holding up as many fingers. "Shelley *who*?" I ask.

We learn that Shelley Harwayne will be in Denver for one week in June, giving a literacy workshop sponsored by the Public Education and Business Coalition (PEBC), a nonprofit group committed to providing ongoing support and leadership for schools in the Denver area. We are required to attend.

Thank goodness! (I say now). What happened that week is hard to explain, but it left me forever changed. I already liked being a teacher, but in just five short days I began to think about children, learning, and teaching in new and exciting ways. I became passionate about my work and passionate about learning, too. It was as though I'd been starving, so insatiable was my appetite to learn more about the kinds of teachers and schools Shelley described.

I started to hang out in bookstores. Don Graves, Lucy Calkins, Connie Weaver, Nancie Atwell, Regie Routman, and Shelley herself had me holed up, reading and writing that whole summer long. I wrote in the margins and dog-eared the pages of books, and I wrote notes and reflections in my brand-new notebook. These authors' words became my words; their visions for teaching and learning became my visions, too. I couldn't wait for school to start!

With the guidance and support of PEBC staff developers Steph Harvey and Pat Hagerty, readers' and writers' workshops were up and running before the first snow fell. Gone were the "If I were a pencil" sentence starters, basal readers, the bluebirds and the redbirds. And gone, too, were the mile-high stacks of stapled work and activity sheets. I had taken, as Shelley called it, "a leap of faith."

Taking their place were literature and trade books, guided and individualized reading, and opportunities for a wide range of responses. Children were reading for longer periods of time than ever before, learning to choose books to read that were just right for them, and flexibly using strategies to figure out unknown words in the context of their reading. Print covered the classroom walls, projects lined the window ledges and spilled out into the hall. Life was good.

But then nagging questions started keeping me up at night. As I planned for the week ahead, I'd wonder, "Am I really teaching kids everything they need to know about reading?" I kept thinking that something was missing; surely there must be something more for them, and me. I discovered I wasn't alone with these thoughts. Some of my colleagues had similar concerns.

As if on cue, enter Ellin Keene. As director of the PEBC's Reading Project, she and other staff developers heard us. Through their collaboration and expertise, a new model of reading began to emerge. Basing their work on reading comprehension research, they showed us that we need to teach children strategies for comprehension as explicitly and with the same care as we teach them about letters, sounds, and words.

I'd found my something more. After years of collaboration with colleagues and work in the classroom, I have visions of my own now. And words, too! The support and love of many have given me the courage to write them down.

To Ellin Keene: you already know I think you're brilliant! Thank you for happily reading drafts over Saturday morning coffee, encouraging me when I became discouraged, and being my friend through it all.

To my friend Steph Harvey, whose passion for learning exceeds that of anyone I know: thank you most of all for teaching me to trust myself.

Thank you, too, for introducing me to Philippa, and for advising me to "cut to the chase" when that's what I needed to hear!

To Anne Goudvis, who gently scaffolded me into the writing world: thank you for your friendship, sharing your wisdom, and helping me with citations at the very last minute.

To Chryse Hutchins: thank you for your encouragement and your insightful work with teachers everywhere.

To Kristin Venable, PEBC staff developer, former teammate, and foremost my friend: now we can go back to Saturday morning coffee at Sisters, walks on the Highline Canal, and baby-sitting, too! Thanks for helping me with computer problems, book organization, and rantings about quitting.

To Kathy Haller: never stop e-mailing me, and thanks for facilitating all those labs. (Maybe we should start one in Vail?)

To Patrick Allen, Leslie Blauman, Mary Urtz Buerger, Bruce Morgan, Carole Quinby, Cris Tovani, and Cheryl Zimmerman, gifted teachers and staff developers who share their work and their classrooms with others on what sometimes seems a daily basis: I'm honored to know and work with you.

To Barb Volpe, Judy Hendricks, and to all those, past and present, whose leadership and commitment have made the PEBC what it is today, I'll always be grateful.

To Philippa Stratton at Stenhouse: thank you for your patience and knowing just when to call and exactly what to say to nudge me forward. (And still it took me forever!) Also thanks to Brenda Power for her kind words and encouragement, Martha Drury for her exquisite sense of design, and Tom Seavey for his marketing expertise.

To Kathy Nutting and many others at Regis University: thank you for a wonderful master's program and for supporting my efforts to make explicit my beliefs about children, learning, and teaching.

To my colleagues and friends at Slavens: you inspire me every day with your wisdom, energy, and love of children, teaching, and learning.

To Barb Smith: thank you for hours of listening, sharing ideas, and responding to my work with honesty. I love that my kids get to go to you for second grade—you always know just where to take them next.

To Michelle DuMoulin: thank you for hosting labs with me and being such a thoughtful teammate.

To Valerie Burke: thank you for your encouragement and for sharing your stash of caramels!

To Sue Kempton: thank you for years of collaboration and friendship.

To Peggy Fuller: thank you for the many things you do for Slavens, especially in the classroom. You lighten my load and let me do what I love most.

To Joy Lowe: thank you, girlfriend, for bringing light and laughter to our school, taking such good care of our kids when we're gone, and teaching us not to take ourselves so seriously.

To Charles Elbot, the principal of Slavens Elementary School: thank you for supporting me in my efforts to write and teach at the same time, and for giving all of us the freedom to teach with our heads and our hearts.

To the parents of Slavens students: thank you for your care and encouragement, for trusting me to love and teach your children well, and for your support of my writing.

To Darby Shaw: thank you for your interest in my work and for being there the day I needed you most.

And kids: I love you! You already know that. But did you know you are the reason I love coming to work? Did you know I learn just as much from you as you do from me? And did you know that it was your smart thinking that helped me write this book? You did? Good job!

To my very own children, Noah and Chad: I love you and am so proud of the young men you have become. Being your mom is my greatest reward.

To Don, my husband and best friend: I love you, babe! Thank you for taking photographs, reading drafts, cooking, cleaning, and shopping so I could write, and having faith in me even when I didn't. And most of all, thank you for loving me, thirty years and counting!

And in memory of my mother, Joyce Everhart, whose own love of teaching never left me wondering what I wanted to be when I grew up.

It Doesn't Get Better Than This

New crayons in bright red baskets sit at the children's tables, flanking caddies filled with sharpened pencils, markers, scissors, and glue. The pencils stand tall, their erasers intact. All sixty-four crayons point in the same direction. Markers fresh from familiar yellow and green boxes have their lids capped tight. And the glue comes out of its dispenser with an easy twist of its orange cap and a gentle squeeze.

A basket of songbooks sits atop the small clusters of tables. Each holds one or two copies of *Five Little Ducks, Oh, a Hunting We Will Go, Little Rabbit Foo Foo, Twenty-Four Robbers, Dr. Seuss's ABC's, My First Real Mother Goose, Chika Chika Boom Boom, The Lady with the Alligator Purse,* and *Chicken Soup with Rice.* Assorted fairy tales, picture books, volumes of poetry, and nonfiction text round out the selection.

In the meeting area, an old floor lamp and several small table lamps glow softly, their shades decorated by children from years past. Plants that have survived the summer are back home on the window ledge; paper flowerpots stick to the windowpanes, waiting for children to paint their bouquets. Empty picture frames await the smiles of this year's girls and boys.

Low bookshelves filled with books sorted into labeled tubs define the meeting area; ABC books sit alongside Arnold Lobel and Henry and Mudge; space and underwater books nestle with the reptiles; and tubs labeled "Predictable Books," "Song Books," "Fairy Tales," and "Little Bear" join "Insects," "Poetry," and "Biographies." Picture books stand tall on shelves of their own.

The Kissing Hand by Audrey Penn, this year's choice for the first day of school read-aloud, stands ready at the chalk ledge. The rocker and the braided rug await us.

The writing table seems to say, "Get over here!" Paper of all sizes and colors, lined and unlined, duplicator and construction, lies straight in organizers that are just the right size. Six staplers and as many tape dispensers line the back of the table, with refills close by. Small containers hold paper clips, pushpins, sticky notes, hole punches, and staple removers. Dictionaries and thesauruses stand at the ready on the ledge behind.

Unifix cubes, pattern blocks, calculators, and bright yellow Judy Clocks; microscopes, magnifying glasses, slides, maps, globes, and atlases fill the shelves in the math, science, and geography areas.

Wooden blocks and Legos left behind years ago by my own children occupy another shelf. Buckets of plastic dinosaurs, insects, reptiles, and other assorted animals are ready for play. Nearby, small tubs labeled "Pastels," "Beads," "Buttons," "Yarn," "Needles and Thread," "Fabric," "Stuffing," "Clay," and "Watercolors" are stocked and ready for work activity time.

Professional books stretch from one end of my desk to the other. Nancie Atwell and Gay Su Pinnell, Donald Graves and Marilyn Adams coexist peaceably. Ellin Keene and Susan Zimmermann, Lucy Calkins, Shelley Harwayne, Georgia Heard, Richard Allington, Brenda Power, Ralph Fletcher, Brian Cambourne, Joanne Hindley, Ralph Peterson, Stephanie Harvey, Anne Goudvis, Harvey Daniels, Connie Weaver, and others join them and are there when I need their counsel.

My plan book is open, all subjects and specials penciled in and accounted for. Paper for individual portraits, first-day interviews, and forms for the Reader Observation Survey and Developmental Reading Assessment are ready to go.

Yellow, orange, purple, and green magnetic letters march across the radiator, spelling "Welcome to First Grade"; the class list is posted in the hall under my nameplate. Sweetheart, Speedy, and Floppsey are fed and their cages pristine. As I take one last look before I leave for the day, I wonder, "Does it get any better than this?"

Twenty-four hours later I find myself under those same clusters of tables, picking up stray Unifix cubes, assorted crayons and marker lids, two butterfly barrettes, an animal cracker, and one small white sock with lace. On the tables, the crayons have abandoned the caddies; pencils are mysteriously dented and have mixed themselves in with the markers, and the glue looks as if it's had more than just a gentle squeeze.

My desk is piled high. Registration forms, emergency cards, testing dates, and memos from the office mingle with money and checks for the PTA, today's lunch, and school sweatshirts. Notes from parents request Girl Scout information, an overview of this year's curriculum, and the date and time of the Halloween parade. Two more parents have written to let me know their children are gifted.

I plop into my chair and take another look. This time I notice the tiny bouquet of dandelions in the red plastic glass, the happy purple, orange, yellow, and green chains that now hang from our doors, and the "I luv U Mlr" written on the dry-erase board.

Magnetic letters that once marched across the radiator now dance, spelling *Mom, Dad, LOVE, Zac, cat,* and *IrNsTPq.*

Yesterday's empty flowerpots hold painted bouquets of what I think might be daisies, roses, geraniums, and tulips. Children's portraits with their too-high-on-the-forehead eyes, crinkled paper hair, glued-on earrings, and bright red lips smile back at me.

I read over their interviews. Hannah wants to learn to write her little letters; Cole wonders why the octopus squirts ink. If they could do anything in the world they wanted, Eric would be a fireman, Will would go to the moon, and Jake would live in the theater district in New York City. When I asked Grace, "What's one more thing I should know about you?" she answered, "You should know I believe in fairies." And Breck's answer? "I really want you to teach me." Now I know for sure. It really doesn't get better than this.

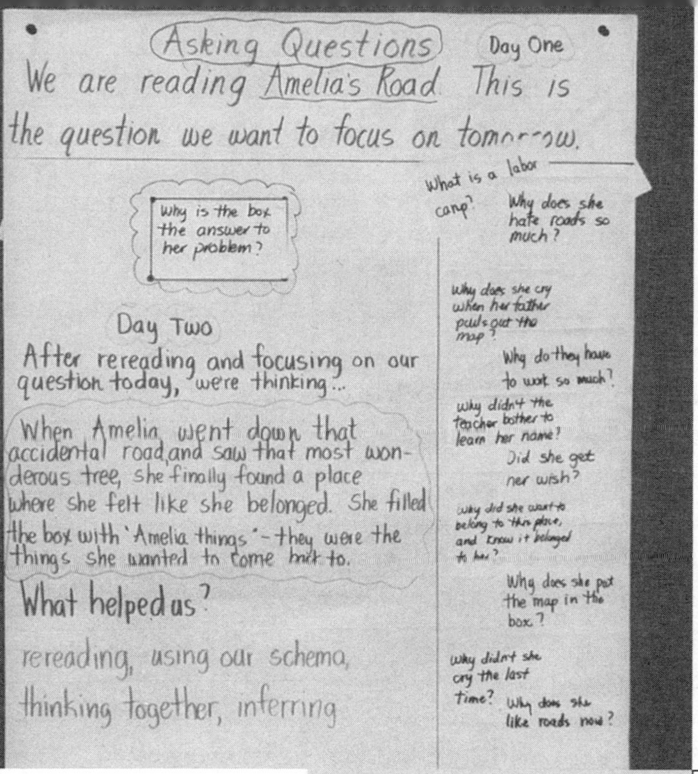

Asking Questions

(handwritten chart)

Asking Questions — Day One

We are reading *Amelia's Road*. This is the question we want to focus on tomorrow.

> Why is the box the answer to her problem?

What is a labor camp?

Why does she hate roads so much?

Why does she cry when her father pulls out the map?

Why do they have to work so much?

Why didn't the teacher bother to learn her name? Did she get her wish?

Why did she want to belong to this place, and know it belonged to her?

Why does she put the map in the box?

Why didn't she cry the last time? Why does she like roads now?

Day Two

After rereading and focusing on our question today, we're thinking...

> When Amelia went down that accidental road and saw that most wonderous tree, she finally found a place where she felt like she belonged. She filled the box with "Amelia things"—they were the things she wanted to come back to.

What helped us?

rereading, using our schema, thinking together, inferring

1
Guiding Principles

Charting children's thinking makes it visible and permanent and traces our work together.

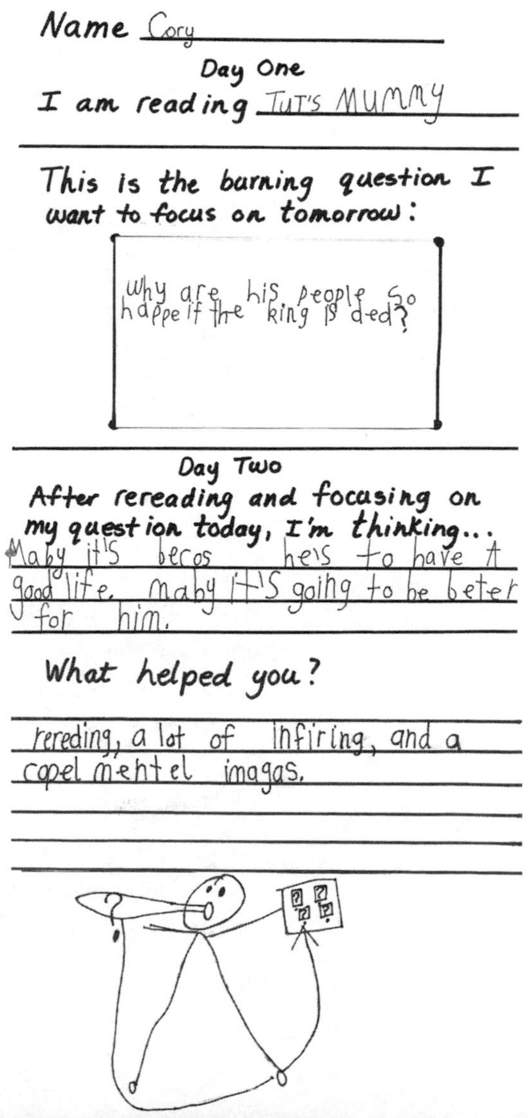

Cory uses the same format for *Tut's Mummy Lost and Found* by Judy Donnelly.

(handwritten worksheet)

Name Cory

Day One

I am reading TUT'S MUMMY

This is the burning question I want to focus on tomorrow:

> why are his people so happe if the king is ded?

Day Two

After rereading and focusing on my question today, I'm thinking...

Maby it's becos he's to have A good life. maby It's going to be beter for him.

What helped you?

rereding, a lot of Infiring, and a copel mehtel imagas.

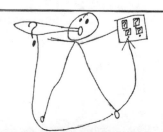

When I think about the principles that guide my teaching of reading comprehension, I realize that they are the same principles that guide my work throughout the day. Gradually releasing responsibility to children as they gain expertise, teaching a few strategies of great consequence in depth over time, and giving children the gifts of time, choice, response, community, and structure guide my work and allow me to make thoughtful decisions based on principles I believe in.

It was Brian Cambourne who encouraged me to make explicit my beliefs about teaching and learning. He supported me and my colleagues at Regis University as we explored the beliefs, theories, and practices of others, considered their implications for teaching in general, tried out new practices in our classrooms, and finally synthesized and made explicit our personal beliefs about teaching and learning.

When we know the theory behind our work, when our practices match what we believe, and when we clearly articulate what we do and why we do it, people listen. At back-to-school night, when I get questions like "Are you phonics or whole language?" or "My child is reading at the sixth-grade level. How will you challenge him?" or "Do you believe in 'invented spelling'?" my stomach no longer churns. I know what to say. No longer are my answers vague, my demeanor tentative, my attitude defensive. No longer do I say things because it's what someone wants to hear. I'm clear. I'm confident. I'm calm. Parents appreciate and respect a teacher who "knows her stuff," even when it doesn't quite agree with theirs.

Or maybe the district is thinking of adopting a new spelling program. I can look at it and know fairly quickly if it's something that I could work with. When an administrator asks us about leveling all the books in our school library or the new assistant principal asks us to dye our hair green if children read a certain number of books, I really don't have to ponder. I know just what to say.

What if you are mandated to do something that you know in your heart is not best for kids? Look at it carefully. Maybe there is a piece of it that will work. As for the rest? Chances are, both your method and the new one have the same goals; maybe you just believe in going after it a little differently. Think about how you believe reading needs to be taught, and be ready to thoughtfully explain how and why. Then make an appointment with your principal and do it. Most administrators listen and support teachers when we speak with conviction, know the research behind our beliefs, and present our point of view in respectful, rational ways.

There are many effective ways to teach children and live our lives. No one has a patent on the truth. Find yours. Read. Reflect. Think about what you already know about good teaching and how it fits with new learning. Read some more. Think about the implications for your classroom. Collaborate with colleagues. Try new things and spend time defining your beliefs and aligning your practices. Once you've found what's true for you, stand up for what you know is right. Live it every day and be confident and clear about why you believe as you do. People will listen!

Establishing a Framework

Think about yourself as a reader. You probably choose what you want to read for a variety of purposes, have opportunities to read for long periods of time, respond mostly through reflection, conversation, and collaboration, and sometimes share your thinking and insights with others. In a readers' workshop, children have daily opportunities to learn to do the same.

Structured around a mini-lesson (15–20 minutes), a large block of time to read, respond, and confer (45–50 minutes), and a time to share (15–20 minutes), the readers' workshop format provides a framework for both strategy instruction and the gradual release of responsibility.

The mini-lesson provides teachers with opportunities to think aloud and show how strategies are used to make sense of text. The large block of time for reading, responding, and conferring allows children to practice strategies in small groups, in pairs, and independently, and gives teachers time to teach, learn, and find out how the children are applying what they've been taught. The share time gives children a chance to share their work as well as an opportunity for reflection, conversation, learning, and assessment.

Sometimes visitors ask me, "You mean you have a readers' workshop every day? Don't the kids get bored? Don't you?" Yes, no, and no. The truth is, I can't imagine having a workshop only two or three days a week, or leaving out a component here and there, depending on my mood. Such questions always draw my eye (and subsequently the visitors') to the quote by Lucy Calkins that hangs above my desk:

> It is significant to realize that the most creative environments in our society are not the ever-changing ones. The artist's studio, the researcher's laboratory, the scholar's library are each deliberately kept simple so as to support the complexities of the work-in-progress. They are deliberately kept predictable so the unpredictable can happen. (1983, p. 32)

To get started, find ninety uninterrupted minutes in your day and put your readers' workshop there. No time like that in the morning? Look at your afternoon. I'd choose a big block of uninterrupted time in the afternoon over a chopped-up morning any day. The workshop won't run ninety minutes until after the first four or five weeks, but teach well and you'll be amazed how quickly your children will get there!

Proficient Reader Research

When Ellin Keene, then director of programs at the PEBC, handed me a copy of the proficient reader research synthesized by Pearson, Dole, Duffy, and Roehler (1992), my eyes glazed over. Who were these guys, anyway? And what did they know about teaching real kids in real classrooms? Yes, I knew something was missing in my readers' workshop. I'd been saying I wanted rigor. And yes, I trusted Ellin. But come on! This stuff seemed way too ivory tower to me.

The article was published in the early 1990s; researchers had spent much of the previous ten years investigating what proficient readers do to comprehend text, what less successful readers fail to do, and how to best move novices toward expertise. From this work, Pearson et al. identified comprehension strategies that successful readers of all ages use routinely to construct meaning when they read and suggested that teachers need to teach these strategies explicitly and for surprisingly long periods of time, using well-written literature and nonfiction.

The research showed that active, thoughtful, proficient readers construct meaning by using the following strategies:

- Activating relevant, prior knowledge (schema) before, during, and after reading text (Anderson and Pearson 1984).
- Creating visual and other sensory images from text during and after reading (Pressley 1976).
- Drawing inferences from text to form conclusions, make critical judgments, and create unique interpretations (Hansen 1981).
- Asking questions of themselves, the authors, and the texts they read (Raphael 1984).
- Determining the most important ideas and themes in a text (Palinscar and Brown 1984).
- Synthesizing what they read (Brown, Day, and Jones 1983).

Sounds simple enough, right? But how exactly does one go about teaching a few strategies of great consequence, in depth, over a long period of time? Especially one who, after wading through the research, is seriously wondering if she is a proficient reader herself?

I was always a fast reader, and therefore, I figured, a good one. In school, I remember being among the bluebirds, flying high through story after story, zipping through the questions at the end, and turning in pages of neatly written seatwork with the pictures colored in just so.

But this stuff was different. What did they mean, think about your thinking? I'm reading too fast to think. Interact with the text? Forget it; I just want to find out what's going to happen next. Draw inferences? Determine importance? Synthesize? I'm not sure what those terms *mean*, let alone know if I do them!

Still, I was intrigued. I wanted to learn more. And because of Ellin, who recognized that the research had merit long before many of us did, small groups of us began meeting once a week to try to make sense of it all. Ellin understood that first we needed to learn about ourselves as readers. She challenged us to be metacognitive—to think about our own thinking as we read. We'd read books and short pieces, keep track of our thinking by jotting notes in the margins, and then talk about the pieces and what we were thinking as we read.

When we began to pay attention to what was going on inside our heads as we read, we were amazed at what we learned about ourselves as readers. We were making connections, asking questions, drawing inferences, and synthesizing information. We began to create working definitions for each of these strategies, realizing early on that the dictionary definition was not going to cut it. (We fancied ourselves way beyond Webster!) While friends chided us to "get a life," we knew Ellin was right. Only when we took the time to really get to know ourselves as readers were we able to seriously consider the implications of the research for the children in our classrooms.

Were we proficient readers all along? I'm not sure. Did all this heightened awareness simply bring to the forefront what was already going on inside our heads when we read? Maybe. Regardless, I'm a different reader now. I've learned to slow down and enjoy the ride; getting there no longer consumes me. Ten years later, I'm still paying attention!

I find myself asking questions, inferring, making connections, and smiling when I silently name what I'm doing. It's not a loud, in-your-face consciousness like it was in the beginning, but a soft, quiet, more natural one, holding conversations with myself when I read.

The proficient reader research has kept me in teaching. Not only was it the "something missing" I'd been searching for, but it systematically raised my expectations for children as well as for learning and teaching. And the best part? Teaching isn't as predictable as it once was. Every day I know children are going to surprise me with their thinking, teach me to see and understand things in new ways, motivate me to think deeply about my teaching, and help me make thoughtful decisions about where to go next and why.

Gradual Release of Responsibility

Chances are that if you think back to a time when you learned how to do something new, the gradual release of responsibility model (Pearson and Gallagher 1983) comes into play. Maybe you learned how to snowboard, canoe, play golf, or drive a car. If you watched somebody do it first, practiced under that person's watchful eye, listened to his or her feedback, and then one fine day went off and did it by yourself, adding your own special twist to it in the process, you know what this model is all about.

Pearson and Gallagher use a model of explicit reading instruction using these four stages that guide children toward independence:

1. Teacher modeling and explanation of a strategy.
2. Guided practice, where teachers gradually give students more responsibility for task completion.
3. Independent practice accompanied by feedback.
4. Application of the strategy in real reading situations.

The table "Components of the Workshop" shows how the readers' workshop provides the framework for teaching comprehension strategies within the context of the gradual release of responsibility instructional model.

Teacher modeling, or showing kids how, includes explaining the strategy, thinking aloud about the mental processes used to construct meaning, and demonstrating when and why it is most effective. Thinking aloud about what's going on inside our heads as we read allows us to make the invisible visible and the implicit explicit.

Guided practice, or what I like to call "having at it" (it is also sometimes called *scaffolding*) consists of gradually giving children more responsibility for using each strategy in a variety of authentic situations. Here, chil-

Components of the Workshop

Phases of Gradual Release	Time to Teach 15–20 Minutes Read-aloud, Mini-lesson Whole Group	Time to Practice 45–50 Minutes Reading, Conferring Small Group, Pairs, Independent	Time to Share 15–20 Minutes Reflection, Sharing Whole Group, Small Group, Pairs
Modeling reading behavior	✗	✗	✗
Thinking aloud (showing how)	✗	✗	✗
Guided practice (having at it)	✗	✗	✗
Independent practice (letting go)		✗	✗
Application on their own (now I get it!)		✗	✗

dren are invited to practice a strategy during whole-class discussions, asked to apply it in collaboration with their peers in pairs and small groups, and supported by honest feedback that honors both the child and the task.

During *independent practice,* or the "letting go" stage, children begin to apply the strategy in their own reading, ideally using real texts in real reading situations. Teacher feedback through conferences is essential; teachers need to let children know when they've used a strategy correctly, encourage them to share their thinking with the teacher and their peers, challenge them to think out loud about how using the strategy helped them as a reader, and correct misconceptions when they occur.

Application of the strategy, or the "Now I get it!" stage, is evident when children apply their learning independently to different types of text or in other curricular areas. By this stage, children are more flexible in their thinking: they begin to make connections between this strategy and others; they can articulate how using a strategy helps construct meaning; and they can use strategies flexibly and adaptively when they read.

So what does all this mean for kids? How can we help them find their own soft and quiet voices? From my reading of the research, late-night and after-school conversations with colleagues, and years of personal experience as a reader and a teacher, I've come to believe that I'm most successful at teaching children to be active, thoughtful, proficient readers and thinkers when I

- have a deep understanding of the strategy being taught and am aware of when and how it helps me as a reader.
- think aloud using high-quality literature and well-written nonfiction.
- gradually release responsibility for using each strategy.
- confer with children regularly and offer honest feedback that moves each child forward based on my knowledge of how proficient readers use the strategy being taught.
- use language that is scholarly and precise, creating a common language for discussing books and ideas both in and out of the classroom.
- teach each strategy separately and in depth, but show how one strategy can build on another.
- teach the reader, not the reading.
- make thinking public by creating anchor charts that children can refer to, add to, or change over the course of the year.
- demonstrate how strategies can be applied to other curricular areas.
- create an environment where reading is valued and seen as a tool for gaining new knowledge and rethinking current knowledge.

How do you begin to plan for a six- to eight-week in-depth comprehension study using the gradual release of responsibility model? First, think big picture. What's your working definition of the strategy you'll be teaching? When do you use it? How does it help you? What do you think is key for kids to know? Next, consider how you will define this strategy. What do you want to say, and how will you say it? Remember, this is a *working definition,* meant to get you and your students started. It doesn't have to be all-encompassing or perfect—the children will help you with that!

Think, too, about what you believe is key to the strategy you'll be teaching. Break it down. What is it that you believe is most important for kids to learn? This book can help you with that, but don't leave all the thinking to me! You'll come up with different understandings that are equally important.

Once you know what you want to teach, think about how you will teach it. What books will you use to model your use of the strategy and the points you want to make? How will you gradually release responsibility to your students? How will you know if they are getting it? For this kind of big-picture, long-term planning, I use a form (shown on the next page) to

Strategy _____

Time frame _____

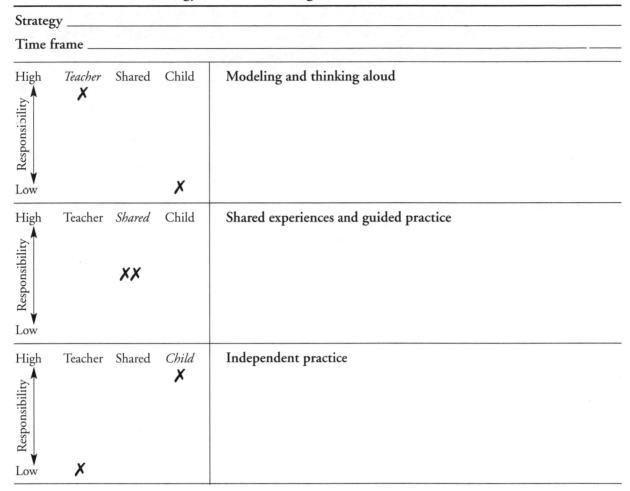

High	*Teacher*	Shared	Child	**Modeling and thinking aloud**
	✗			
Low			✗	

High	Teacher	*Shared*	Child	**Shared experiences and guided practice**
		✗✗		
Low				

High	Teacher	Shared	*Child*	**Independent practice**
			✗	
Low	✗			

help me think about where I want my students to go and how I hope to get them there.

I know it's difficult just to think about planning a six- to eight-week course of study—in fact, I used to think it was counterproductive. After all, how could I possibly know where we'd be eight weeks from now? But this isn't about the day-to-day planning—that still needs to be done. Rather, this "big picture" planning is about creating a well-thought-out, *overall* plan that guides my work and gives direction to my day-to-day planning.

There's nothing worse than walking into school each morning having to figure out what to teach, scramble for a book, come up with a plan. When we get caught in that trap, our teaching becomes disconnected, just a series of lessons rather than a coherent plan for learning.

Do I ever deviate from the big picture? Absolutely. I never know when a child or a colleague will cause me to think about things in new ways, lead me in new directions, and redefine my old thinking. As David Pearson said, "Good planning, like good instruction, is as intentional as it is adaptable" (Pearson, personal interview, 1995).

"Books are lovely" by Frankie Clifford

Frankie's response to the question "What do we know about books?"

2

In September

Sharing a snack is the perfect time for practicing good manners and the civility of conversation.

15

It's late afternoon. The children have gone for the day, and save for a lone cricket chirping from his bug box in a faraway corner, the room is quiet. It's the second week of school, and despite vows that this year it's going to be different, that this year there really will be balance in my life, I'm already feeling overwhelmed and out of sync. And instead of being smart and heading out for the gym, or even staying to get ready for Wednesday's Back to School Night, score the district's newest assessment, or check my voice mail for the messages I know await me, I find myself watching the sunlight as it streams in through the windows.

My eye catches a stack of letters peeking out from under a pile of books. Realizing they're the ones I'd asked parents to write, and mortified I'd forgotten them in the rush of the first week, I sink (or is it slink?) into the once-white overstuffed chair in the corner and begin to read.

I'd invited parents to take a few moments to write me about their children, asking them to think about things that might be important for me to know as well as their hopes and expectations for the coming year. As I read, I learn that this year's children are animal lovers, Irish step dancers, Kenny Loggins enthusiasts, pianists, creative artists, Lego-maniacs, gymnasts, soccer players, geniuses, and budding geniuses. They are dubbed silly, smart, sweet, caring, serious, mature, young, sensitive, gregarious, shy, confident, playful, and imaginative.

Matthew's parents write that from the day he was born, he had a sparkle in his eye, and now they do, too. They say that "more than anything, Matt would love to read." Caitlin's family tells me they waited ten years for her and that she is "the light of our lives." And Danny's parents write, "we moved into the neighborhood because our dearest wish was for you to be his first-grade teacher." (Yikes!)

As I read the letters from the parents, I'm struck by the love between the lines, the hopes and dreams that live in their words, and the faith and trust they have in me. No one wrote that they wanted their child to score high on the Iowa Test of Basic Skills, or attain Level 20 by the end of first grade, or even meet the highly publicized state standards. It's not that they don't want those things for their children, but the things they chose to write me about—the things they considered most important for me to know—were not about test scores, reading levels, or state standards.

I remind myself that in the incessant push for higher test scores, and in the face of endless editorials about the demise of public schools and misguided politicians and their plans for reform, I must not let myself—or my budding geniuses—get caught up in some kind of frenzied, frantic pace that knows no end. I remind myself not to let go of what I know is best for kids. For me, September is all about building relationships, establishing trust, creating working literate environments, and getting to know children as readers and learners—and remembering that our classrooms still need to be joyful places where we take the time to appreciate Matthew's sparkling eye, Isabella's shy poetic spirit, and Kendal's boundless energy.

Community: Creating a Culture and Climate for Thinking

If you had asked me about the importance of creating a sense of community in my classroom ten years ago, I'd have said it was everything. I'd have talked about the interviews and surveys we do at the beginning of the year, the self-portraits taped above the chalkboard, the photographs everywhere of children playing and working together. I'd have told you about Talent Show Tuesdays, about writing and signing "Our Promise to Each Other," and about the children's work that hangs not only on the boards and doors but also from the wires that crisscross our room. I'd have told you about the cozy spaces where children work in small groups, pairs, and independently, and about rituals for birthdays, losing a tooth, and saying good-bye. And finally, I'd have mentioned that each day begins with our singing "Oh, What a Beautiful Morning" with Joanie Bartels, and ends with an a cappella version of "Happy Trails to You" written by cowgirl Dale Evans.

And if you asked me about the importance of creating community today? I'd still say it's everything. But now I know that once the promises are written and signed, the room beautifully and thoughtfully arranged, and the photographs taken, developed, and sitting prettily in a frame, our work has just begun. Real classroom communities are more than just a look. Real communities flourish when we bring together the voices, hearts, and souls of the people who inhabit them.

When our vision of community expands to create a culture and climate for thinking (Perkins 1993)—when rigor, inquiry, and intimacy become key components of our definition—it's essential that we work *first* to build genuine relationships, establish mutual trust, and create working literate environments. If we look to the months ahead and envision children constructing meaning by spontaneously engaging in thoughtful conversation about books and ideas, asking questions that matter to them and exploring their solutions, and responding independently to a variety of text in meaningful ways, we must be deliberate in September.

Building Relationships

I begin by paying attention to the little things. It's noticing Paige's cool new haircut, Grant's oversized Avalanche jersey, Kendal's sparkly blue nail polish, and Cody's washable tattoos. It's asking about Palmer's soccer game, Jane's dance recital, Elizabeth's visiting grandpa, and Hannah's brand-new baby brother.

It's giving Ailey a heart rock to add to her collection, copying a poem about cats and giving it to Gina because I know she loves them, and even putting a Band-Aid on Grace's tiny paper cut. Showing children we care about them and love being their teacher is an important first message. And at the same time, I'm modeling for children how to show someone you care about them; I'm modeling how you go about creating lasting friendships.

Teaching children how to listen and respond to each other in respectful, thoughtful ways also helps foster new relationships and caring communities. I used to have long conversations with children about this, telling them how important it was to listen carefully to each other and to really think about what their classmates have to say. I'd talk about responding respectfully, to look at the person you're speaking to, call them by name, and on and on. But the very next day a child might groan at a song another had chosen, wildly wave a hand when someone else was talking, or flip through the pages of a book while another child was sharing. And I'd go into the whole respect routine again. During these conversations, the children were just as eloquent. They *sounded* just like me! But their behavior didn't change. And I'd wonder, "What's going on here? Why don't they get it?" And even sometimes, "What's wrong with these kids, anyway?"

Eventually I realized, of course, that nothing was wrong with "these kids." They didn't get it because I hadn't *shown them how*. I'd *told* them to be respectful, thoughtful, and kind, but I hadn't shown them what that looks and sounds like.

The best opportunities to show kids how occur in the moment. When Frankie says to Colleen, "Colleen, could you please speak up? I can't hear what you have to say," I can't let that pass without making sure everyone heard. I can't let that pass without pointing out how smart it is to want to hear what someone has to say. I say, "You guys, did you just hear Frankie? Frankie, could you say that again?" She does, and I ask, "So boys and girls, why was that such a smart thing for Frankie to do?" They respond, and then I use their words and mine to bring our thoughts together.

And when Max tells Jack that his idea is "a little bit dumb," I can't let that pass either. I say, "Max, I'm sure you didn't mean to be rude to Jack, but when you said his idea was a 'little bit dumb,' that's what *you* were being. It's okay to disagree with someone, but there are nicer, more polite ways to do it. You might say something like, 'Jack, I don't understand what you mean' or 'Jack, why do you think that?' Try it again, Max." He does, beautifully this time, and I don't miss the opportunity to let everyone know how much we've learned from Max today.

Or Sean is trying to find a place in the circle, and he starts nudging himself into a spot four inches wide. I say, "Sean, could you think of a better way to get yourself into the circle?" Sean's stumped. "Well, how about this? The next time you need to be in the circle and there isn't room, how about asking someone to scoot back so you can fit in? Let's try it right now. Just say, 'Sunny, could you please scoot back so I can fit in the circle?'" He does. Next, I turn my attention to Sunny. "Okay, Sunny, Sean has asked you nicely to scoot back. What could you say back to him?" She says, "Sure, Sean, I'll scoot back for you." With smiles all around, she does.

Is the first time the charm? No. And probably not the third time either. But remain diligent. Remain calm. Don't give up the good fight! Once the flagrant violations are in check, watch closely for the rolling of eyes, the private conversations, the exasperated sighs. Don't let those go by either.

You can use these first lessons—we can call them "anchor lessons"—to refer back to. For example, when Sarah snaps at Troy, I say, "Oops, Sarah, what's another way you could tell Troy what you're thinking? Think back to how Max handled something like this." We'll assist her if she needs it, but a gentle reminder is usually enough.

Here are a few more teachable moments.

To the children with the wildly waving hand when someone is talking: "You know what, guys? I know you're not meaning to be rude, but when your hand is up and someone else is talking, I'm thinking you're probably focusing on what you're going to say rather than listening to the person who is speaking. What do you think? Since we can learn so much from each other, remember to keep your hands down and really listen and think about what your friends are saying. When they're finished, you can share what you're thinking."

To the children who abruptly get up in the middle of a story or discussion: "Oh my goodness, you're going to leave us *now*? Think of the learning you'll miss! Can you wait until the story [or discussion] is over? Thanks."

To the children who always have something to say, no matter the topic or the day, and the ones who hardly have anything to say, ever: "Today I want you to think about yourselves as listeners and speakers. If you're someone who's great at talking a lot, I want you to be a listener today. See what you can learn. If you're someone who is a great listener, I want you to do some talking today. We want to know what you are thinking, too. Raise your hand if you think you do a lot of listening. Raise your hand if you think you do a lot of talking. Wow! You really know yourselves. That's so smart. Let's try it."

To those who have already heard every book in your library and can't wait to let you know the minute you hold it up: "That's so great you've heard this book before. And you know what? Since we know how much more we can learn and understand when we reread, I want you to pay special attention when you hear the story today. Think about what you notice this time that you didn't notice before. Think about what puzzled you the first time, and what you think about that this time. Will you let us know?"

Doesn't all this take a lot of time? You bet. But it sets the tone for learning and thoughtful conversation; it paves the way for the work that lies ahead. Once children realize you're not going to relent, once they realize that this is not just a "sometime thing," and once they understand what you want them to do and why it's important, it becomes habit. It becomes part of the language of the classroom.

Establishing Mutual Trust

Like building relationships, establishing trust takes time. And it must begin with me, the teacher. Every time I value a child's idea by acting on it, think out loud to make sense of a question or response because I really want to understand, or ask children what they think and then listen carefully, I let them know I respect their thinking and trust that they have something smart to say.

I don't mean in a superficial "they're only seven" kind of way; I mean trusting children enough to give them the time and the tools to think for themselves, to pose and solve problems, and to make informed decisions about their learning. Respecting their ideas, opinions, and decisions doesn't mean carte blanche acceptance, but it does mean giving their voices sincere consideration. Trust needs to be mutual. If we're asking children to thoughtfully consider the thinking of others, we must expect no less from ourselves.

It was Lauren who made me a believer. It was early in her first-grade year, and she'd been happily reading books like *Whose Mouse Are You?* by

Robert Kraus and *Cookie's Week* by Cindy Ward. But the day I read aloud Mary Hoffman's *Amazing Grace,* things changed. She had to have that book. I gave her my usual line: "You know, Lauren, I'm thinking this book is too challenging for you right now. How about waiting awhile, then giving it a try? You can keep it safe in your cubby until then. Let's find *Where Are You Going, Little Mouse?* I think that would be perfect for you." But she'd have none of the mouse. It was *Amazing Grace* she wanted.

In the end, she won me over. But once I'd said yes, I couldn't just give her the book and say, "You go, girl." Once I'd relented, I needed to do everything I could to help make her decision—now ours—a good one. I had to figure how best to support her and maximize her chances for success. This wasn't about power or proving a point; this was about helping a little girl learn to trust herself and make good decisions about her learning.

We made a plan together: I'd help her learn a page a day at school, she'd reread what she'd learned already, and she'd take the book home every night to practice. Five weeks later, the kids and I were calling her Amazing Lauren! And she was amazing. Not only was she able to read *Amazing Grace,* but she was off and running, reading books like *Oliver Button Is a Sissy* by Tomie dePaola, *Wild Wild Wolves* by Joyce Milton, *The Paper Bag Princess* by Robert Munsch, and *Honey, I Love* by Eloise Greenfield.

What if I'd said no? Would she have learned to read *Oliver Button, Honey, I Love,* and the others? Probably. But I want to do more than teach kids how to read. I want to teach them how to go after something if they really want it, I want to teach them the rewards of hard work and determination, and I want to teach them that if they're sincere, I'll do everything I can to support them.

If we expect big things from children, we must expect big things from ourselves, too. For years I'd been told what to do in my classroom and how to do it. Glossy teacher's guides with smiling children on the cover even told me what to say. I didn't always read the words in italics *exactly* as written (I considered myself a rebel even then), but I'd get the gist of the lesson from the guides. Beyond running off worksheets and making cute activities for centers, I never had to think much about reading at all. Come to think of it, the kids didn't either.

So when PEBC staff developer Steph Harvey blazed into my room with a whole new way of thinking about children, learning, and teaching, she made my head hurt. Every other week she'd come, lugging a tote bag so full of books they left a trail behind her like Hansel's crumbs of bread. She'd do a fabulous demonstration lesson, we'd debrief over lunch, and then off she'd go. "Wait!" I'd plead. "Can't you leave me with a bit more of a plan until you come back?" Just like my teacher's manual, I wanted her to tell me where to go next; I thought she knew more about my kids than I did.

But Steph was wise. She wouldn't hand over any prescribed set of mini-lessons. Instead, she'd say, "Come on, Deb. Think about what you already know about good teaching. You know your kids. Where do *you* think they need to go next?" Her best advice? "Trust yourself."

Only when I began to assume responsibility for the teaching, learning, and *thinking* in my classroom did I understand that I really did know my kids, what they needed, and where they needed to go next. Only then did I begin to believe I was smart enough to figure this stuff out for myself. I'd had support from Steph, yes, but she'd made it clear the decisions were mine to make. She'd trusted me before I'd known to trust myself.

And because she did, I wanted to live up to her expectations; I wanted to be as good as she thought I was.

Actually, I wanted to be even better. I began to read more professional books and articles, to join study groups, and to observe other teachers. I worked long hours defining my beliefs and aligning my classroom practices; I came to know the supporting research. I learned to believe in myself.

So what are the implications for the children in our classrooms? They're huge. When we show children we expect them to share thoughtfully in the responsibility for their learning, when we let them know we believe they're smart, and when we support them just enough so that they'll be successful, we're doing for them what Steph did for me. We're trusting them first so that they can learn to trust themselves.

In my role as staff developer, teachers and others often observe our readers' and writers' workshops. Invariably, someone will come up and whisper, "You know, they really are talking about the book back in the corner over there." (They think I'm going to be surprised.) Or they'll wonder, "So how do you know what your kids are doing if you don't meet with each one every day?" and "You mean they can just go up to the library all by themselves?" I tell them what I've already told you; later we talk about getting started.

Start small. Think about the things in your classroom that you do automatically, without even thinking why. Ask yourself, "What am I doing now that I could trust kids to do?" and "In what ways could I trust children where I haven't before?" Think about things like . . .

Do they really need to go to the bathroom and get a drink all at the same time, or could children take care of those things on an individual basis? Do I need to count and monitor the number of pretzels or animal crackers they take for snack, or can I trust them to take two or three? Am I the only one capable of refilling the staplers and tape dispensers, and replacing sticky notes, worn-out markers, and paper towels? Do I really need elaborate and time-consuming check-out systems for books, CDs, markers, videotapes, calculators, or whatever else children may want or need at home? I say no. Not when we're clear about what we expect and why. Not when we trust kids enough to show them how.

Torin and Jack work together to sound out words.

3

Readers' Workshop:
Real Reading from the Start

Real literature by real authors engages young readers.

The voice of Joanie Bartels singing "Oh, What a Beautiful Morning" is the signal for children to finish selecting their books and gather in the meeting area. By the last "I've got a beautiful feeling, everything's going my way," everyone's singing along with Joanie. Readers' workshop in first grade is in full swing. We've been at it for almost three weeks now, and children have learned how to select their books for the day, how to gather for a story and mini-lesson, how to practice reading behaviors in authentic situations using real books, how to use workshop procedures, and how to share with their classmates what they've learned about themselves as readers.

"Hold the phone," you might be thinking. "How could they learn all that in just three weeks?" or "How can you have a readers' workshop when they can't even read?" Hang on. The fact is, most children haven't learned to decode or comprehend. Not yet. And still, they see themselves and their classmates as readers. They clearly look the part, and right now, that's precisely the point.

Readers' workshop in September is less about teaching children how to read and more about modeling and teaching children what it is that good readers do, setting the tone for the workshop and establishing its expectations and procedures, and engaging and motivating children to want to learn to read. Once these are in place, we can move forward quickly without the distraction of management, procedural, and behavioral issues.

Rigorous environments do not have to be rigid or restrictive. I know we have mandates, time lines, and important tests to give. And still I say slow down! Learning to read should be a joyful experience. Give children the luxury of listening to well-written stories with interesting plots, singing songs and playing with their words, and exploring a wide variety of fiction, nonfiction, poetry, and rhymes. Let them know when they say or do something smart; give them credit and ask them to share. Help children access what they already know and figure out how to help them make connections to something new. Be genuine. Laugh. Love. Be patient. You're creating a community of readers and thinkers; you're building relationships and establishing trust. Come October, you'll be glad you did.

Book Selection: In the Beginning

Remember the red baskets of books sitting atop children's tables I mentioned earlier? For the first two or three weeks of school, children select their books each day from these. I include a variety of books in the baskets, mostly the songbooks we've been learning, but also familiar fairy tales, ABC books, a few picture books, poetry, and well-illustrated nonfiction. I add new song-books to the baskets as we learn them, favorite read-alouds, and sometimes enlarged, photocopied, laminated copies of poems, songs, snippets of text, or rhymes children especially love. Each basket (ours are the 12-by-18-inch plastic ones) holds around twenty-five books and serves four to six children.

In September, the books and materials I've chosen are most likely not at the children's instructional level; whether a child can or cannot read them doesn't matter right now. I've chosen them because the familiar songs and story lines, the short text, and the colorful illustrations are perfect for chil-dren's working with books, practicing reading behaviors, becoming engaged and motivated, and building community.

When children arrive each morning, they select three or four books from the basket at their table, place them at their seats, chat a bit with their friends, and begin reading. In a couple of weeks, children may choose to sit almost anywhere in the room, but in the beginning, when we're establishing procedures, reading behaviors, and the tone of the workshop, they sit at the tables. I use this time to say hello, have brief conversations with the children about what's going on in their lives, and offer reassuring words to the few par-ents who still have a hard time saying good-bye. I also do some noticing (love those bright red sneakers!) and check to see if anyone needs help with book selection. After most of the children have arrived, I put on the music and chil-dren gather in the meeting area for the day's read-aloud and mini-lesson.

The tone for the beginning of the school day has a relaxed, social, "I'm glad you're here" sort of feel. It's very similar to the way I begin my own day; I can't imagine walking into the building, striding down the long hall to my room, unlocking my door, and immediately creating a chart or reviewing the day's lessons. First I need to feel connected in some way to the people I work with, whether it's asking Sue about her new baby girl, talking with Barb about the class we teach together, or stopping in to check out Michelle's tadpoles and chatting about why hers are again twice the size of mine. I need to take the time to light a candle, put on a little Eric Clapton or Keb Mo, and ease myself into the day.

Reading Aloud

My first read-aloud is almost always a songbook. I introduce a new song-book each day, I have two or three favorites ready to go, then I ask for requests. Most days we end up singing six or seven—children love the predictable text, rhythm, and rhyme. This continues well into October, and while we might "graduate" from *Five Little Ducks* by Raffi and *Oh, a Hunting We Will Go* by John Langstaff, we begin the day with music all year long. Often I'll type up the words to favorite songs from CDs, tapes, books, and my Girl Scout days. The children follow along, and once they know the words, laminated copies go into the baskets and plain copies are sent home.

In addition to their repetition, rhythm, and rhyme, my reasons for choosing songbooks and singing songs are many:

- They're fun!
- Children are instantly engaged and motivated to learn to read the words. I have multiple copies, and children can't wait to get their hands on them.
- The words and tunes are easy to learn; children read along right away and feel part of the "reading club" almost immediately.
- They build community. Where else would "Little Rabbit Foo Foo" be declared "our song"?
- Children love to take them home to share with parents, brothers, and sisters. I send a note with the copies, telling parents the purpose of the songbooks, ways to support their early reader, and reassurances that yes, right now, pointing to words and memorizing are good things! Parents appreciate being connected to the classroom so early in the year, and sometimes respond by sending in words to songs they learned as kids.
- Repeated readings increase phonemic awareness and build sight word vocabularies.

Once we've warmed up with songbooks, I read aloud one or two other types of books, depending on their length and the children's mood. Sometimes I'll read one of the books out of the baskets at the children's tables; I try to vary genre, author, format, and style and think about books this particular group of kids can easily connect with or what might pique their interest.

Reading aloud comes into play throughout the day. After lunch and/or at the end of the day, I often read aloud from a chapter book. Perennial favorites include *The Trumpet of the Swan* by E. B. White, *Mr. Popper's Penguins* by Richard and Florence Atwater, *Pippi Longstocking* by Astrid Lindgren, *Poppy* and *Poppy and Rye* by Avi, and the My Father the Dragon series by Ruth Stiles Gannet.

Reading aloud is one of the most important things I do. I can't believe I used to feel so guilty about it that I'd shut the classroom door! Now I know reading aloud motivates kids to want to learn to read, extends their oral language, and gives them opportunities to connect new information to what they already know. And reading aloud offers teachers opportunities to

- share a variety of genres.
- model fluency and reading behaviors.
- construct meaning through think-alouds and offer children the time and tools to do the same.
- build community.
- share with kids our love of reading and learning.

Mini-Lessons

At the beginning of the school year mini-lessons focus primarily on modeling and identifying reading behaviors and teaching and learning the expectations and procedures of the workshop. Reading behaviors are the observable things that readers do—the deliberate actions we take that connect us to our lives as readers. Think of them as the habits we keep, like keeping a running list of books we want to read, recommending books to friends, participating in book groups, or even bookmarking our places with a paper clip or rubber band. If we want children to develop habits that readers keep, we must heighten their awareness by explicitly modeling and pointing out what it is that readers do and giving them time to practice these behaviors in authentic situations using real books. Focusing first on what readers do prepares children for learning *how* they do it.

A first lesson on reading behaviors could begin this way: "Boys and girls, from talking with you and reading letters from your parents, I've learned that this is a class that wants to learn all about reading. Is that true? It is? Well, guess what—I love to teach kids all about reading, so this is going to be perfect! I'm thinking that you guys are like a lot of other kids I know: I'm thinking that you know a lot of things about reading already. Let me show you what I mean. Think about somebody you know who loves to read. Can you get a picture of that person in your head? Good. Now, this person you know who loves to read, what do you see him or her doing? What do you know about this person as a reader?"

Children respond:

"They have book clubs; my mom's in one with Oprah!"
"They go to the library all the time and check out a ton of books."
"They read lots of different stuff, like my dad. He reads newspapers
      and books and magazines and papers from his work."
"They read a lot."

"Listen to you!" I tell them. "You *do* know a lot about what readers do!
I'll record your words on sentence strips like this one, and then I'll tape
them on the door there. That way we won't forget. Over the next couple of
days, let's do some investigating—let's watch carefully for people who are
readers and notice what else they do. Let's see how many more things we
can add to our list."

At the end of the week, the door is covered. Children and I observed
readers

"talking about books and ideas."
"recommending books to each other."
"asking questions about the stories."
"reading with friends."
"trading books with each other."
"pointing to the words as they read."
"rereading books."
"buying books."
"sounding out words."
"laughing, crying, smiling, frowning."
"reading out loud."
"using a bookmark."
"finishing one book and starting another one."
"writing on Post-its and sticking them in the book."
"looking at the pictures and reading the little words under them."
"reading really fast."
"reading slowly."
"looking up a word in the dictionary."

Children also started paying attention to where readers read, and they
insisted on recording this information, too (on another door). So, where do
readers read?

In bed
Under a tree

On the porch
Up in a tree house
Under the covers
In school
At a soccer game
In a bubble bath
On an airplane
In the bookstore
At the checkout stand
In the car
Waiting in line
On the couch, and
In a big red chair!
(I think we have the makings of a poem here!)

From the first lesson on, I model and children begin practicing the things that readers do, and we talk about the reasons why. For example, one day we might begin a series of lessons on what readers do when they finish reading a book. From discussion and our class-generated list, we learn that they might reread the book, choose another one, talk about their book with a friend, or read it with a buddy. We also speculate (and soon find out first-hand) why we might do each of these things. For example, we might choose to reread to better understand the story, get better at reading the words, get ready for a book group, or maybe just because we love the book.

Because the list of reading behaviors is long, I choose the most important behaviors—that is, the ones I think are most important for beginning readers to practice early on. I put my energy, and theirs, into those.

What's my purpose here? Why spend time modeling and practicing reading behaviors? I've learned that doing these things

- sets the tone for creating a working literate environment.
- lets children know that they share in the responsibility for their learning.
- builds community—together we investigate, learn, and practice what it is that readers do.
- offers kids opportunities to make informed choices about their learning.
- fosters independence.
- actively engages readers early on and builds confidence.
- sends the message, "You are smart, I know you can do this, I'll show you how."

Mini-lessons this early in the year also establish workshop (and classroom) procedures. I begin by asking myself just two questions: What are the things that consistently interfere with teaching and learning? and What procedures can be put in place to lessen or eliminate their impact?

What drives me crazy? It's the grinding of the pencil sharpener when children are working, the plaintive voices asking to get a drink or go to the bathroom, children lining up or calling out to ask how to read or spell a word. It's being interrupted during a conference with a child or a conversation with an adult, transition times that take too long, children telling me, "I'm done," or asking, "What do I do now?" It's kids' abandoning books without making the effort to have a go, my asking for their attention over and over, and announcements over the intercom about candy sales, Brownie meetings, and the band.

What keeps me sane? If the problem can be solved in the classroom, I quickly initiate conversations and/or mini-lessons about what it is that's interfering with teaching and learning, why it's a problem, and how we might solve it.

A procedural mini-lesson might begin this way: "You know, yesterday I was conferring with Cody, and all of a sudden we heard the loud, grinding sound of the pencil sharpener. Do you know the sound I mean?" Their nods and big eyes tell me they do. "It seemed to go on forever, and Cody and I couldn't focus on our work. We couldn't even remember what we were talking and thinking about. Right, Cody? And I'm wondering, did the pencil sharpener interfere with anyone else's learning?" Tales of woe follow.

"I have an idea that might help us—let me know what you think about this. See these two cans? One is labeled 'I'm sharp!'; the other is labeled 'Please sharpen me.'" If your pencil lead breaks or it gets dull from so much writing, put it in this can labeled 'Please sharpen me.' Then, just take a sharpened pencil from this one, the 'I'm sharp!' can, and keep working. What do you think?" Everyone thinks it's a very smart idea.

Another day during reading, two children behind me keep repeating my name, another is softly tapping my shoulder, and one more is doing something with my hair. I turn and face them. "Hey, you guys, I'd love to talk with you, but I'm in the middle of a conference. Please find a place to read quietly, and right before we share we'll talk about other ways for you to let me know you need me when I'm working with someone else. Be thinking about what might work." Then, during the "How's it going?" part of the share, I say, "Girls and boys, before we begin sharing, there's something we need to talk and think about. I know there are times during reading when you really need to talk to me and I'm busy conferring with someone else. I do want to help you, but I can't just stop in the middle of a conference. What do you think we could do to make this better? Take a couple of minutes to talk with those next to you and see what you can come up with."

Jake and Olivia propose that "if there's something that only Mrs. Miller can help you with, you could write her a little note and stick it on the dry erase board. Then keep on reading until she comes to you; don't just, well, you know, sit there." Olivia reminds everyone to "sign your name." After the initial flurry of messages, we agree: it's a hit.

Why not just post a list of rules on the first day of school and be done? I remember those days, but that was when the room was mine, not ours; that was when I was the only teacher, and they were the only learners; and that was when I asked all the questions, and had all the answers, too.

Reading and Conferring

Before sending children off to read, I'm explicit about what I want them to do, how they can go about doing it, and why it's important. I want them to begin this part of the workshop with a clear sense of purpose; I want them to be thinking, "I get it. Now let me have at it!" So how do kids "have at it" when most are not yet reading? Reading books and working with books are two different things. Although learning to read and comprehend books is our goal, working with books helps get us there and introduces children to the real world of reading.

Let's say the mini-lesson had been on using sticky notes to mark the places in your book where you learned something about yourself as a reader. Before sending the children off, I'd say, "In your reading today, if you find yourself thinking, 'Hmmm. I just learned something about myself as a reader today—I figured out the words *space* and *suit* by looking at the picture,' remember to mark that page with a sticky note, just the way I showed you. That way, you can keep track of your learning and thinking, *and* if you share, you'll know the exact page to open your book to. Got it? Good. Think, too, about *why* marking your learning and thinking is an important thing for readers to do. Let's talk later about what you discovered during the share. Happy reading!"

I know that not all children will keep track of their learning and thinking by marking the text with sticky notes today, but some will. The enthusiasm and excitement generated by even one or two children as they model and share how it helped them as readers and learners are contagious.

Okay. Let's say you agree with the importance of reading aloud, and you're comfortable with mini-lessons. But sending kids off to read and work with books so early in the year? What would that look like with twenty-seven first graders? Well . . . It's Jamie and Grace singing "Five Little Ducks" over in a corner while Jane's carefully pointing to the words I've copied onto chart paper and Torin and Palmer are looking at a book about snakes, gleefully poring over the bulge that has got to be an eaten mouse. It's Brodie and Frankie, each signing out a copy of *The Lady with the Alligator Purse* by Nadine Bernard Westcott and *Chicken Soup with Rice* by Maurice Sendak— they have a play date after school and already they're making plans to make Rice Krispies Treats and read in Brodie's tree house. It's Sheldon, Cain, and Conner wandering a bit—how many drinks have they had? Cole's in a corner following the tiny black-and-white drawings in *Hand Rhymes* by Marc Tolon Brown, trying to manipulate his fingers and read "Two Little Monkeys" at the same time; Grant's working at my desk with *Touch the Poem* by Arnold Adoff, making a list of every word he knows—already he's up to seven! Nickie's just read *It Looked Like Spilt Milk* by Charles Green Shaw three times and *Twenty-Four Robbers* by Audrey Wood twice, and now she's searching the basket for a copy of *Little Rabbit Foo Foo* by Michael Rosen. It's Julianna and Jake, giggling and marking their pages with sticky notes every time they figure out a new word, their books overflowing with the bright yellow flags of their learning. Troy's snuggling in that once-white chair leafing through *Dr. Seuss's ABC's,* singing the alphabet song to no one in particular. And at one table, Jamie's reading all about Henry and his big dog, Mudge; it looks like Colin's coloring circles on sticky notes and putting them in his book, *Gemstones* by Ann Squire; and Colleen has spread out three different versions of *The Three Little Pigs,* comparing illustrations and story lines.

What am I doing in the midst of all this? I'm conferring with children, taking notes, and learning as much as I can about them as readers. I'm intrigued by Colin: what's with all the colored circles on his slips, and what has this very social little boy so engaged?

"Hey," I say, sliding up a chair. "Colin, it looks like you're really into that book. Can you talk with me about it?"

"Well, I think it's a really good learning book for me."

"What do you mean, a really good learning book?"

"Well, I always like to learn new stuff, and I like rocks and this book gets me to know more stuff about 'em."

"Like . . ."

"Well, you see here on this page—" he finds the slip on which he's drawn a red circle, "see, on this page, it's all about rubies. Red, red rubies."

"That's so smart. How did you know this page was all about rubies?"

"See?" He points to each letter. "R-U-B-Y, that says *ruby*. And here's a picture of a ruby. It's red. And here it says *red,* see, R-E-D."

"Ruby, that's kind of a tricky word. How did you figure it out?"

"It's not tricky! It's my grandma's name!"

"That's funny! Do you see any other words on this page that you know?"

Colin squints. "Let's see. Um, there's *the,* and *see,* and oh! There's *ruby* again!" More squinting. "That's all for today."

"Good reading, Colin. Thank you. You know what else? I'm so interested in all your sticky notes with the colored circles. How does that work?"

Deep breath. "Okay. So say I want to learn about rubies, I just put my finger right in front of the sticky note and open it up. See? And here's where the blue rocks are, and the purple ones, and the green ones. Get it?"

"I do get it! That's so smart to mark your place that way. I'm thinking that would be a smart thing to share with everyone. Would you do that? Share with them what you shared with me?"

"Sure!"

"Thank you for talking with me, Colin. I learned a lot from you today! See? I wrote it all down here. Look at all you know!"

"What's it say?"

"It says that you like nonfiction books—they're the kind that give you information, like *Gemstones.* And that you're confident—that means you believe in yourself and try new things. Here it says you can work with other kids, like you did yesterday, and by yourself, too, like today. And here? See these words? These are the words you read to me. Want to read them again? . . . Good job! And these words next to the star? I wrote a note to myself to try to find some other books about precious stones or colored rocks for you; some that have fewer words on a page. All these things show me how smart you are, and help me know how I can teach you best. Did I get everything?"

"Did you write that my grandma's name is Ruby?"

"Oops! I forgot that. I'll put that right here, next to the words you know. Before I go, do you need my help with anything?"

"I want to know the names of all the rocks, like the purple ones, the green ones, all the different colors. Will you teach 'em to me?"

"I'd love to teach them to you! Why don't you pick two or three right now? We could make a book that has all the names of the gems you know during work activity time if you'd like. We could keep adding to it every time you learn a new one. What do you think?"

Huge grin. "I want to know this purple one."

"That's an amethyst." I write the word under the purple circle on his sticky note.

"And this green one."

"That's an emerald." I write *emerald*.

"Do we really get to make a book during work activity?"

"We do."

"Will you write it down in your notebook? With a star?"

"You bet."

"This is the best day of my life! Hey, Colleen, I get to make a book all about colored rocks in work activity!"

Colleen raises an eye. "Well, I'll still be studying *The Three Little Pigs*."

"So, Colin," I say, "what will you do next?"

"I'm just gonna stick with this book, and next I want to read *Way Down South,* this one right here."

"Good plan. Thanks, Colin. Bye."

"Adios."

I slide my chair over to Colleen. "Hi, Colleen, what's going on over here? . . ."

Sharing

I signal that share time is about to begin by singing, "Everybody listen!" Children sing back, "Right now!" I ask them to think about what they've learned about themselves as readers today and to think a minute about how they might best share that with the group. I slip a CD into the player, and before the final chorus of Rosenshontz's song "One Earth" children have arranged themselves in a large circle and are singing along. Some have books in front of them, indicating they'd like to share.

This part of the workshop has evolved over the years into more than a time for children to share their learning. It's that, for sure, but some days it's also a forum for exchanging ideas and discussing issues, making connections from our reading lives to the world, and constructing meaning for ourselves and each other, one idea at a time.

In September, much of our time is spent setting the tone and establishing procedures. While I'm interested in what children have to say about what they've learned about themselves as readers, I'm not focusing so much on the *content* of what they have to say right now. I'm not worried when their thinking seems muddled or off the mark—that's natural. Right now I want them to practice oral language and the civility of conversation; I want them to know how it feels to think about their thinking; I want them to become familiar with the routines and procedures of the share.

Because I know that some of the most significant learning will come from this part of the workshop, it's important that I make clear what the sharing will look and sound like, and why. Once again, I think about what I want for kids in March, April, and May, and set about getting them there.

I know I want children to be reflective and thoughtful not only about books and ideas, but also about how they view the world and their place in it. That's why we spend the first few minutes of the share reflecting on the day so far. I ask them to think about questions like "How did reading go for you today? What's working well for you?" and "What's not working so well?" When a chorus of children answers the first question with, "Good!" (they always do), I know I've got work to do! I'll say, "Think back. What was good? What about today was good for you? Can you think out loud about that?" Then I give them time to formulate their answers. Or maybe I've asked, "Is there anything that didn't go well today?" and a child answers, "It was too noisy for me." In that case, I respond with, "What was too noisy? How did it get in the way of your learning? Think back and think out loud about what we could do to make it better tomorrow."

Children don't always know that they know something. My modeling, guiding, and nudging them to think back, think out loud, and take a reflective, thoughtful stance often show them that they do. Later in the year, when I ask them, "So how do you know?" or "What makes you think that?" or "Tell me more about your thinking," they've had practice being reflective and thoughtful. The time we spend thinking out loud about the day sets the tone for the rest of the share. Children come to understand that I expect a respectful, thoughtful, time-to-listen-and-learn-from-each-other frame of mind.

I model and talk with children about their responsibilities for sharing, listening, and learning. Every day I remind them, "If you'd like to share, remember you need to be prepared: bring your book, think about how you can best share your learning, and speak loudly enough so that everyone can hear." I tell the rest of the children, "If you're the ones who are learning, you'll need to be looking at the person speaking, listening carefully, and thinking about what he or she has to say. Is everybody ready?"

I take a look around the circle and notice those who want to share. I usually begin with children I've conferred with that day, particularly those who I know have something pertinent to share (most likely this means something connected to the mini-lesson). I invite children by saying something like, "Colin, would you like to share?" Colin answers, "Yes, thank you. The title of my book is *Gemstones,* and when I was reading today I did this really cool thing. See all these Post-its? If I want to study about rubies, I find the red circle—that's the color rubies are—and I just open it up to this page. If I want to study the purple rock, it's called a—um, what is it, Mrs. Miller?"

"It's called an amethyst."

"Yeah, *amethyst*. If I want to study about them, I go to the purple circle and open up to this page. See? And we're going to make a book at work activity and I'm going to learn to read all the names of every one in the book."

"Colin," I ask, "can you talk a little about how you're using the Post-its to help you as a reader?"

"Um . . . they help me find my place so I don't have to take forever trying to find stuff?"

"You've got it! Thank you, Colin. Boys and girls, what did we learn from Colin today?" Hands fly.

Jamie, Grace, and Jane each have a copy of *Five Little Ducks* in front of them. I invite them to share, and they begin singing.

"Oops!" I say. "What do you need to say back? Let's start again. Jamie, Grace, and Jane, would you like to share?"

"Yes, thank you," they answer together.

"Perfect. Now, tell us about what you're going to do, and what you learned about yourselves as readers."

Grace begins. "Well, we learned all of the words in *Five Little Ducks,* and we want to sing for everyone. You can clap, but only at the end." They sing, and we clap at the end. After a brief lesson on clapping (how long is too long?) I ask them, "So, how did you get so good at reading the words? What did you learn about yourselves as readers?"

Jamie nails it. "We kept practicing and practicing. And we learned that sometimes it's fun to learn a book together."

Grant shares the ten words he already knows from his book today. He thinks writing them down on sticky notes is a good idea, but he's not sure how it will help him as a reader. I'm not sure, either, but Olivia knows. "Now he's learning to write the words he can read." "So what do you think, Grant? What do you think about what Olivia said?" Grant smiles and gives a little shrug.

People who visit often say to me, "That's so cute how they say, 'Yes, thank you.' How did you get them to do that?" Maybe it is cute, but that's not why I ask the children to respond that way. It's about tone, it's about respect, and it's part of the language we use as we live and learn together for six-and-a-half hours every day. Later in the year, visitors ask, "How do you get your kids to talk and share their thinking like that? My kids could never do that." How did I get them to do that? It's really pretty simple. I taught them.

To	From	Title	Why?
Stephnie	Sarah	GOOD WORK AMELIA BEDELIA	you like the caracter!
Margret	Charlotte	The animal Rescue Club	You Really Like Animils
Alben	Charles	Reb WolF COUNTRY	You LICK WolF and I ThE The books to FarWOLF
Marin R.	Marin W.	A mare for young Wolf	it is full of advenchers...
Emma	Tory	Cinderella	youre a fairy tale gal!
Margaret	Ellie	Dancing with Manatees	Becas you Lice Laerning
Kevin	Ben	NOISY poems	YOU LIKE Silly poems
Marin W.	Breanna	Just For you	It is Fany
JULIET	Margaret	POCAHONTAS	You LIKE TO BE FREE TOO
Ian	Kate	THE YUcKy REPTILE	You LICK LRAEning aBOUT Reptils
BEN	KEVIN w.	COLORFUL chameLEOMS	You Like Nonfiction
David	Mrs. Miller	Mouse Soup	You like stories like these!

4

Settling In

Asking children to think about why they're recommending a book to a friend encourages thoughtful recommendations.

Camille chooses to read (and fingerplay) Marc Tolon Brown's *Hand Rhymes* during readers' workshop.

39

The zucchini is piling up in the teachers' lounge. Halloween costumes and giant bags of bite-sized candy bars have replaced wading pools and charcoal briquettes at the local KMart. And I'm just about ready to admit that yes, this year's group has potential! Readers' workshop has taken on a new look, too. By late September, children understand its procedures and expectations. They know all about *what* readers do; now they're ready to learn *how*.

Book Selection: Theirs

Because my goal is for children to apply strategies for decoding and constructing meaning independently, it now becomes essential that *most* of their books be at their instructional level—"just right." It's difficult to apply strategies when you know every word and understand everything; it's equally difficult when you know hardly any words and understand very little. Pulling just any book off the shelf or out of a basket will not do.

Even so, giving children choice is important. I could easily hand each of them a book or two that I think would be just right, but why? Teaching children how to make thoughtful book selections is hard work, but it's not out of their reach, or ours.

Early mini-lessons on book selection should focus on the ways readers make good choices. Much of the word on the street has to do with matching kids with books based on such features of text as vocabulary load, sentence length, amount of print on a page, and predictability. I also teach children to consider

- the size of the print: Is it too little? Too big? Just right?
- the words and lines on a page: Are there too many? Too few? Just the right amount?
- the pictures: Do they seem like they will help me read the words?
- repetition: Is a predictable text what I need?
- the words: Can I read all of them? Most of them? None of them at all?

In my years of teaching children how to make thoughtful and appropriate choices, however, I've learned there's more to book selection than readability. If we mean it when we say we want children to become lifelong readers, if we mean it when we say we want children to actively engage in text for a variety of purposes and for increasingly long periods of time, we can't teach them to make book selections based on readability alone. If we really mean it, we *also* need to teach children to pay attention to

- Content: What's my schema for this? What do I know about this topic or story?
- Schema: What do I know about myself as a reader and the books in the classroom to help me make a good choice?
- Motivation: How hard am I willing to work to learn to read this book? (Remember Lauren, the mouse, and *Amazing Grace*?)
- Variety: Have I selected more than one type of text and level of difficulty?

Content

We all know kids who have extensive knowledge about a specific topic. Adam is this year's dinosaur expert—he's been passionate about them since he was three. Now he's six, and he's found his way over to the dinosaur tub. I don't know the level of the book he's chosen, but it's clear it's way too difficult for him according to traditional leveling guidelines. As I confer with him, I learn that not only can Adam read the word *dinosaur,* but when I teach him how to activate and apply what he already knows about dinosaurs, he can also read words like *triceratops, stegosaurus, plant eater, asteroid,* and *millions of years ago*. Because he knows so much about the topic and his motivation is high, he's able to read a book of greater difficulty than a traditional assessment might indicate.

Think, too, about children who know about certain types of stories. Caroline, Devon, and Nicole, like Adam and his dinosaurs, know fairy tales. Because these stories have a language all their own, it's no surprise that with only a little nudging, they can read words like "Once upon a time," "Who's that sleeping in my bed?" "Not I," said the pig," "Trip, trap, trip, trap," and "I'll huff and I'll puff, and I'll blow your house down!" The story lines are so well known to them that they can navigate text that, based on readability alone, would appear too challenging.

Schema

When we begin to talk about using schema, or prior knowledge, to comprehend text, it makes sense to talk with kids about combining what they know about themselves as readers and what they know about the books available to them in the classroom to help them make thoughtful choices.

One day I might read four or five books from the tub labeled "Learn to Read." I'll point out things I notice as I read, and after reading several volumes in this series, children begin to join in with things they notice, too.

When I've finished reading, I'll ask, "So, what do we know about these kinds of books? Let's make a list of what we know to help us remember." I write "Learn to Read" at the top of the sheet, record the class's thinking, and tape the sheet on the wall above the tub. In the days to come we do this for six or seven tubs of books. Throughout the year, children assume responsibility for researching other tubs of books as they build schema for new series, authors, or types of text.

I also ask, "What kind of a reader would this type of book be best for? Do you think these books would be smart choices for kids just learning to read, those who have had a little more practice reading, or someone who has been practicing a long time? Why?" We decide that because the print is large, the songs, rhymes, and stories are familiar, the text is predictable, and the pictures match the words, the "Learn to Read" books would be good for kids just learning to read or for someone wanting to read something that's short and fun.

Connecting what children know about the books in the classroom to what they know about themselves as readers helps narrow their selections. When a child knows that he is just starting to read, and that the "Ready Set Read" books usually contain familiar fairy tales, with only a few sentences on a page, attractive pictures, and big print, he knows right where to go. Or if a child is a more fluent reader, and she knows that the "Frog and Toad" books are about two friends and their adventures, and that the books have quite a few words on a page and a few pictures, she'll know she'll be interested.

Motivation

What was it about the story *Amazing Grace* that so motivated Lauren to want to read it? Her story is not as unique as it once was. Now I know more about the power of the read-aloud and the discussions that ensue, the value of student choice, the importance of creating literate environments that are purposeful, accessible, and organized, and the significance of teacher attitudes and expectations.

When I read aloud a favorite book to children, I'm doing more than reading a good story. I'm showing my love and enthusiasm for reading and learning, I'm sharing my thinking and inviting children to join me, and I'm encouraging and expecting students to do the same in their reading. My message is clear: I love reading. I know you will, too. Let me show you how.

Children know I'm not going to ask them to do something beyond their capabilities. I want them to succeed, and I offer recommendations that are just within their reach. And because they trust me to know them well, they respond in ways that sometimes surprise both of us. Success begets motivation.

Visitors to our classroom sometimes wonder how children as young as six, seven, and eight can sustain reading for forty-five or fifty minutes a day. When children understand that they share in the responsibility for their learning, when they have a say in the books they read, and when what they are asked to do has meaning, they are able to read for long stretches at a time.

When children recommend books to each other, share their thinking and learning at the end of a workshop, or sign up as an expert on the "Want to learn to read a new book?" chart, they motivate each other. When several children decide to tackle a challenging text together, stay in the meeting area after a read-aloud to reread parts of a text and take the day's conversation deeper, they set the standard for thinking and learning in the classroom.

Variety

Can you imagine reading only professional books, only poetry, or only the books on the Oprah table? I can't either. But what about limiting kids to only one level and/or type of text day after day? That's hard to imagine, too. I worry when we methodically move children through book after book, level after level, all to achieve some target number that labels them—and us—proficient.

I worry about their engagement and enthusiasm for reading and learning, I worry about their concluding that reading fast is reading well, and I worry about losing the Adams, the Carolines, the Devons, and the Nicoles along the way. Readers of all ages need a variety of text type and level of difficulty.

How do I teach children how to thoughtfully select a variety of text that meets their needs as readers? I begin by bringing in the odd assortment of reading that's stacked beside my bed. I show them the Pottery Barn catalog and the dog-eared page that shows the quilt I'm thinking of ordering for my son Noah. I hold up my book group book, *Flags of Our Fathers,* and share some of what I've written on the sticky notes jutting out everywhere. They see my *Language Arts* magazine, and the article where I've highlighted parts I want to remember. I show them *I Read It, but I Don't Get It,* by Cris

Tovani; *This Same Sky, A Collection of Poems from Around the World* selected by Naomi Shihab Nye; and a book called *The Hours* recommended to me by my friend Chryse Hutchins.

I talk about how some of my reading is *easy* for me, like the catalog; *just right,* like *Language Arts, Flags of Our Fathers,* and *I Read It, but I Don't Get It;* and challenging, like *The Hours* and many of the poems in the poetry book. I point out the variety of text I'm reading—a magazine, a catalog, a nonfiction text, poetry, and fiction—and my reasons for choosing them.

Then I say, "Let's take about fifteen minutes right now to make new book selections. Think about choosing a variety of books, both in the type of text you are choosing and the level of difficulty. Think about whether they are easy for you, just right, or challenging. Remember, readers mostly read books that are just right, but you could decide on an easy one or a challenging one, too. Think about what you know about yourself as a reader *and* the books in the classroom to help you make good choices. Last of all, make sure you are able to talk about *why* you've made the choices you've made. Let me know if I can help."

Twenty minutes later, the children are seated in a circle, their stacks of books in front of them. They're eager to share their selections. Everyone is browsing through the various choices; many are sharing their books with each other. This is exactly what I'd hoped for. I love it when I have a stack of new books to read, and I want the children to feel the same way.

To help everyone focus I ask a question: "Griffy, would you like to share your books, and tell us why you chose them?"

"Yes, thank you." Griffy holds up *Little Bear's Friend* by Else Holmelund Minarik. "Well, you see, I got this one because I've read all the other Little Bears, and this is my last one. Little Bear Books are just perfect for me. And then this one, *Mouse Soup,* Mrs. Miller gave it to me because she thinks it's just right for me, too, and it's funny and she knows I like funny ones. I got this one, *Tough Boris,* because I have lots of schema for pirates. It's cinchy for me, but I still like to read it. Let me show you my favorite page! I got *Mouse Tales* because it looks sort of like *Mouse Soup,* and it was in the same tub so it's the same author—there's lots more in there if you want one, too. And then I found this huge book about space. See?" He struggles to lift the heavy text. "I know a lot about space. This book looks like fiction but it's really nonfiction, and it's about the planets and all that stuff we're learning about. Remember about Venus, and how it's the hottest planet? It shows how the gases are all trapped up, see, right here? The words are very tiny and hard for me, but it's still good for me."

"Wow, Griffy," I say, "you made some very thoughtful choices! What do the rest of you notice about Griffy's book selection?"

I believe children need to spend their time reading appropriate text—and I believe we need to broaden our definition of what's appropriate. Singing and pointing to the words of "Long Tall Texan" with a friend, looking at a shark book and learning from its pictures and captions, and reading *Hush Little Baby* by Sylvia Long because you've been working hard and need a break, are appropriate choices, too.

Now that I've modeled and the children have practiced many of the ways readers make good choices, how else might I support children as they choose? How else might I ensure that most of their chosen books are at their instructional level? I take an active role. What's most effective?

Book talks. About once a week, all year long, right before the mini-lesson, I showcase three or four books that I know will be just the right match for specific children. I read the title and the first three or four pages, and I browse out loud through the book. Then I say, "You know, Matt, I'm thinking this book might be perfect for you. Would you like to give it a try?"

Sticky notes. If I know a child might not like a public recommendation, or if I find a book before or after school that I think would be a good choice for a child, I often write a personal message on a sticky note, place it on the cover, and put it in the child's cubby. I might write, "Hi, Nicole! I saw this book and thought of you. It's another version of *The Three Billy Goats Gruff.* Let me know what you think of it. Love, Mrs. Miller. P.S. Who's that tripping over my bridge?"

Read-aloud. Remember to read aloud some of the titles children are reading, too. Not only does it elevate the status of the book *and* the status of the child you recommend it to, but it also gives children a preview of the text. Once I've finished, I'll say to a child I know would benefit from reading the book, "Grant, would you like to try this one?"

Recommending charts. Though I certainly do my share, I'm not the only one doing the recommending! Children love recommending books to each other. To facilitate this process, I divide a large piece of chart paper into three columns headed "To and From," "I Recommend," and "Why?"

Go looking together. Sometimes a child just needs you to take him or her by the hand to several tubs that you know would offer good choices. Browse through the books with him, thinking out loud about the kinds of things you want him to be thinking about when he begins to choose independently.

Pick one. Offer three choices, all of which you know are just right. Ask the child to pick one.

Conferring. Conferences are the best time to talk with children individually about books and book selection. If a child is making consistently poor choices, you can talk about why these choices are not going to help her become a better reader, and recommend some that would. When you make recommendations, think out loud about why you think these books would be just right.

For example, to Sean, who is comfortable reading *The Lady with the Alligator Purse* by Nadine Bernard Westcott, *Little Green Frog* by Beth Coombe Harris, and *The Bear Went over the Mountain* by Robert Bingham Downs day after day, I say during a conference, "Wow, Sean, you really know these books. How did you learn to read them so well?" He says, "I just kept practicing." I say, "That's so smart. And you know what? I think you're ready for something a little more challenging. You know how you can read all the words and you understand everything that is going on? That tells me you're ready for some books that will help you become an even better reader. Are you up for a challenge?" The slight nod gives me the go-ahead. "Let's go look at the tub of 'Start off Stories'—do you remember where they are?"

Sure enough, he leads me to the "Start off Stories" and we have a seat on the floor. "Remember these books?" I say, pointing to the tub and the "What do we know about 'Start off Stories'?" sheet taped above it. "They have a few more words on the page than your other books, but you have schema for lots of them already. The pictures match the words, and the text is predictable. And you're not going to believe this, but some of them are fairy tales, and I know you like those. See? Here's *The Little Yellow Duck*— it's kind of like *The Ugly Duckling*. And here's *The Ant and the Dove*—it's a good story, too. You want to try *The Little Yellow Duck*? Wow, I love it when kids are up for a challenge! That's so smart." At this point I'm thinking, "Come on, Sean, I'm the one doing all the thinking here! Are you listening?" But I say, "Let's read a little of it together. . . ."

I check in on Sean now and then to see how he's doing, and I ask him if he'd like to share what he learned about himself as a reader today. He declines. Unwilling to let the opportunity pass—both for him and for other kids who could learn from him—I say, "You did such a smart thing today, Sean. Would you mind if I shared how you tried something new?" He relents, and in the end decides to do it himself. At share time, Sean tells the class, "Well, today I got a new book, and here it is. I didn't think I could read it, but Mrs. Miller thought I could, and I can. I'm going to practice it some more." (Hey, maybe he *was* listening!)

■ ■ ■

Once we decide that it's important for children to have a say in the books they read, not only must we teach them how to make wise choices, we must also make available high-quality selections that offer a wide variety of levels, topics, and types of text. This probably sounds as though I have a huge collection of books in the classroom. I do. But it hasn't always been that way.

Check out your school and local libraries. They almost always have great children's collections, both for reading and thinking aloud and for independent reading. Get to know librarians—they can be wonderful resources, and they'll often let you check out large numbers of books for long periods of time if they know your purpose. Borrowing books from libraries also lets you try them out first and decide which ones you might want to own or order.

Be choosy. Build your collection slowly. For thinking aloud, look for high-quality literature that is likely to prompt thinking and discussion, has believable, compelling characters, and deals with real childhood issues, especially complex ones. When we believe it's important for children to construct meaning by interacting with the text and developing personal perspectives, we must select books that give them the opportunity to do so. Childhood is not all happy, not all sad, not all good, and not all bad. Don't be afraid to let kids know you know this.

Be choosy about what you select for kids to read independently, too. You don't like Captain Underpants or Scooby Doo? Don't let them invade your classroom! Children should be reading well-written books that promote thinking and have believable, compelling characters who talk the way real people talk and do the things real people do.

Many first graders would give their eyeteeth (if they had them) to read chapter books. I do have a few in the room, but even if the children can read them, I don't encourage them to do so—picture books are often better written and more thought-provoking for young readers. And besides, what's the rush? Children have years and years of chapter books ahead of them.

Beware, too, of the giant boxes of books dropped off in the lounge from the Kiwanis Club's annual book drive. I know they mean well, but do we really want our children learning to read with someone else's old basal readers, Walt Disney's cartoon versions of the classics, pop-up books that no longer pop, or picture books scribbled on by a three-year-old long since grown? Yes, there will be treasures. Just don't get into thinking all books are equal. Just like the outcast computers that come our way, quality really is better than quantity!

Evaluation: Mine

Most schools require some sort of baseline assessment of children's reading skills at the beginning of the year, and mine is no exception. In first grade we use the Reader Observation Survey developed by Marie Clay and the Developmental Reading Assessment (DRA) to evaluate early literacy achievement. The survey assesses letter identification, concepts of print, sight words, writing vocabulary, and dictation. The DRA measures a child's reading level through running records and retellings.

We administer the Reader Observation Survey as needed and the DRA at the end of the year as well as at the beginning, in order to give teachers, children, and parents a clear indication of how children have grown as readers in the areas mentioned above. But how do we measure a child's developing expertise in other areas of reading comprehension? It's very different than evaluating a child's skills in decoding. I can't give comparative levels or numbers to parents and say they represent how their child has grown in his or her ability to comprehend. I can share what I've learned from children during conferences, observations I've written in my notebook detailing what I've seen and heard the children say, and artifacts that show how children acquire new knowledge and construct meaning.

You'll find examples of these kinds of responses in the "Evidence of Understanding and Independence" sections at the end of each strategy chapter. These sections include a wide range of artifacts—children's work, their comments and strategy definitions, and classroom charts we've constructed together. You'll notice that examples of comprehension ability or development aren't tied directly to a child's ability to decode. A child with few decoding skills can make an amazingly complex inference while reading a beginning picture book. Likewise, a child who is an accomplished decoder may struggle to make even the simplest connections from his reading to his life experience. You'll notice from the syntax and spelling in the classroom artifacts that the children are clearly beginning readers, yet they are able to use their developing comprehension skills in sophisticated ways.

I've experimented with many different ways of record keeping, and have finally settled on small 4-by-6-inch notebooks that I keep in a basket near my desk. There is a notebook for each child, and every day before our literacy workshops I scoop up four or five from the front of the basket. Throughout the work sessions, I confer individually with these four or five children and make notes about what I've learned about them as readers, writers, and learners.

Entries might include words the child wrote on a sticky note, oral responses, a quick running record, and/or strategies the child uses for decoding and comprehension. I also make note of a child's specific strengths and areas where he or she needs more support. Listing specific examples from conferences and observations keeps my comments real and in context, and puts me back in the scene when I need to refresh my memory.

At the end of each week or so, I look at these notebooks, along with notes from my own notebook and the children's response sheets, and determine if there are children with similar needs who would benefit from additional support. I meet with small, needs-based groups for fifteen to twenty minutes during the independent practice part of the workshop. Small groups may need additional instruction, modeling, and practice making relevant connections, sounding out words, or working with vocabulary development. Or a small group may need to challenge themselves by choosing more sophisticated texts, applying a strategy in a new genre, or sharing their thinking and learning with others.

In these lessons children most often use the same text, but I also ask them to bring a book they are reading independently. We use like texts so we have the same point of reference; they bring the books they are reading independently so we can make a plan for independent practice. In the lesson, I model what I want them to practice, and we discuss why it's important.

Small groups like these give children opportunities to teach and learn from each other as they work together to apply and practice strategies for comprehension, decoding, and meaning of words. We chart our learning and children share their new insights during share time. Groups stay together for one, two, or three work sessions over a one- or two-week period. I meet with just one small group a day as needed, ensuring time to confer with individual children, too.

What About Phonics and Word Identification?

My focus in this book is on helping children develop strategies for comprehension. But you might be wondering how children learn about letters, sounds, and words. Some believe it's not wise to teach young children strategies for comprehension while they are still learning to decode. I believe these strategies should be taught side by side.

In *Comprehension Instruction: Research-Based Best Practices* (Block and Pressley 2002), Pearson and Duke write that "'comprehension instruction' and 'primary grades' should appear together often—that comprehension instruction in the primary grades is not only possible but wise and beneficial rather than detrimental to overall reading development" (p. 247)

Children love to learn about words and are fascinated by their growing ability to use them in new ways. To capitalize on this enthusiasm, I use the same strategies for teaching words as I use for teaching comprehension. Explicit instruction, modeling, reading high-quality literature and children's writing, and giving children time to practice real reading and writing are the cornerstones of my teaching. I find that much of the work we do is integrated into our whole-group discussions, small-group meetings, and independent practice sessions every day.

I use the morning message as an opportunity to teach and reinforce earlier lessons on sentence structure, vocabulary, and strategies for decoding. I record a couple of simple sentences on the dry-erase board, such as "Good morning everybody. Cory's mom is coming in to help us today. We will be working on determining importance, and we get to explore our new books about the solar system." We investigate these words and sentences in a variety of ways. We might focus on identifying sight words, recognizing spelling patterns, finding little words in big words, chunking sounds together, or learning word meanings—all using the morning message.

Singing breathes life into the classroom and provides opportunities to investigate words, letters, and sounds. When the whole class is gathered on the rug, and we sing "Dr. Seuss's ABC's," the children learn the names of the letters and the sounds associated with them. When children listen to stories, I explain what they can observe about concepts of print and language, how stories are structured, and how to figure out the meanings or words. Or I give children copies of songs we've learned and ask them to point to the words as we sing, matching voice and print, associating letters and sounds, and building sight word vocabularies.

In small-group meetings, we often work with spelling patterns or word families. We begin by talking about a particular spelling pattern, such as *ight*. I find several examples in a couple of books and, after discussing the words, I send the children off to collect their own words with the same pattern. We chart and share our learning. When children recite and read nursery rhymes, play with tongue twisters, and read snippets of text I've retyped from favorite read-alouds, they develop a sense of the predictability of language, the repetitive nature of words, and the relationships between letters and sounds.

Children have daily opportunities to learn about words and sentences during independent reading and writing. They learn about sound-symbol relationships and features of words when I ask them to write down all the sounds they hear when writing independently. Every moment children spend reading independently is a time to apply what they know about words in a real, relevant context. I often transform the snippets of text I've retyped from favorite books and songs into cloze activities. By eliminating several nouns, for example, or even omitting every sixth or seventh word from the text, I encourage children to use their developing knowledge of syntax to fill in the blanks that make sense and sound like language.

I make a point to stop with the class on the way to the lunchroom to read a few words or sentences from a third grader's pond project or point out the words they already know around the lunchroom. When we're on our way to a field trip, the children revel in showing me the words they know from every billboard and fast food restaurant we pass. I know that they are acquiring a sight word vocabulary they will build on for a lifetime.

While introducing children to the fascinating quirks and essentials in the world of words, I try to remember that a real context in reading and writing is just as important when I am teaching comprehension. The most

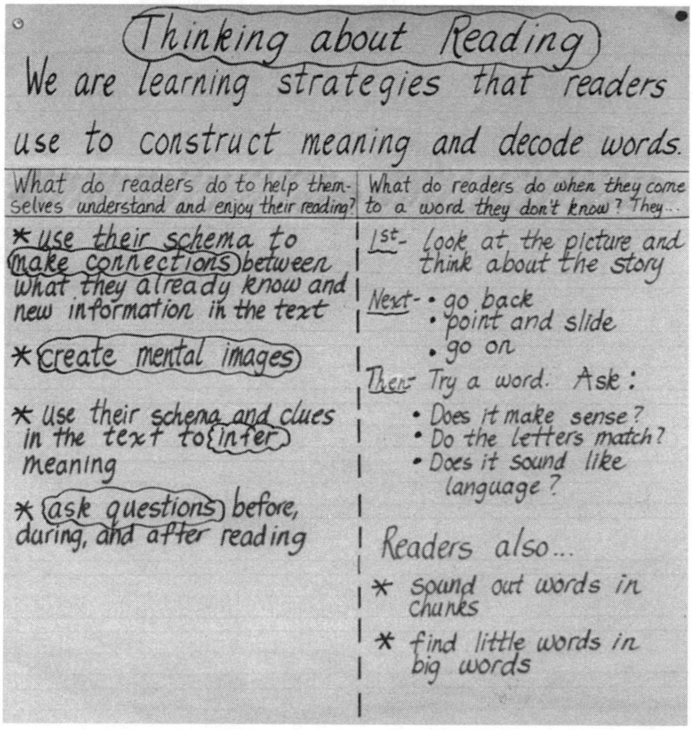

FIGURE 4.1 An in-progress classroom chart that shows the side-by-side teaching of decoding and comprehension

effective ways to teach comprehension are also the most effective ways to teach words. I model, think aloud about how I use particular strategies to figure out unknown words, and list our learning on chart paper. I use a variety of literature as well as the children's writing, and I encourage the children to think aloud during share time about their success in pronouncing words they never thought they could.

To emphasize my belief in the side-by-side teaching of decoding and comprehension, we have a chart in the classroom titled "We are learning strategies that readers use to construct meaning and decode words" (see Figure 4.1). The chart is divided into two columns: "What do readers do to help themselves understand and enjoy their reading?" and "What do readers do when they come to a word they don't know?" We add new learning and information to the chart throughout the year.

A reminder to help children make thoughtful and appropriate book selections is always a good idea.

5

Schema

Choosing a new book?

Use your schema about books AND what you know about yourself as a reader to make a good choice.

Children combine what they know about decoding and comprehension as they read and think about text.

53

It is early October, and I'm getting anxious. "Are they ready?" I wonder. Twenty-seven first graders sit together on the carpet in our small meeting area. The lamps are lit, the Pumpkin Spice candle is burning, and my lesson is ready to go. I scan the crowd. Kenta has his hands inside his bright orange Bronco shirt. Bret is braiding Maggie's hair. And Whit is rolling his socks down, up, then down again.

My mind flashes back to last year's class. "Were they ever like this?" I wonder. "Will this group learn to read as well, and think as deeply?" I remember what my husband said when I ran this by him the night before. "You say the same thing every year," he told me, "and then in November, you can't believe how smart they are." With his words in my head, I begin.

Thinking Aloud: Showing Kids How

I thought that once I became aware of the thought processes going on inside my head as I read, modeling this activity—thinking out loud while reading a picture book to first graders—would be a piece of cake. Not exactly . . .

I cringe when I think of one particularly awkward attempt, using Eve Bunting's book *The Wall.* Colleagues had told me what a fabulous book it was, and I lost no time grabbing it off the shelf of my local library. I flipped through its pages that night at home, unsure of what I'd say as I read, but oddly confident that something would come to me.

Nothing did. The next morning in class I heard myself rambling on, unsure of what to say and making things up as I went. Flustered and embarrassed, I realized from this experience that no longer could I continue to blithely read away, making a comment about beautiful language, throwing out a question or two, sharing a random connection. No longer could I grab just any book off the shelf just because it had been recommended to me, or because it was written by an author I knew and loved. The bar had been raised. Now, when I model the thought processes proficient readers use, I'm deliberate. I make sure my think-alouds are genuine, my language precise, my responses thoughtful. Here's how to make that happen.

Proper planning prevents poor performance! Explicit modeling requires thoughtful planning. We all know of times in our teaching when we've been able to "wing it," and sometimes these lessons turn out to be our most brilliant. But "winging it" to model our thinking as we read is difficult to pull off. Ask yourself beforehand, "What do I want kids to understand about this strategy? Of all the places in the text where I could authentically think out loud, which two or three would best illustrate my point? Which ones am I most comfortable talking about?" Mark those places before your lesson, and think about what you will say and how you will say it.

Resist the temptation to talk your way through a lesson or figure it out as you go. Being absolutely clear about the one point you're trying to make helps drive it home. For example, if the lesson is on making text-to-text connections, you won't need to share those places where you have questions, or even text-to-self connections. Be aware of your focus and keep it.

Authenticity matters. I can't fake it. My connections, or questions, or inferences—whatever the strategy focus happens to be—must be genuine. That's why book selection is key; choosing well-written picture books, narrative and informational nonfiction, and poetry that you love and can use over the course of a year to model a variety of strategies is essential. No matter how perfect someone else may tell you a book is, or how great a lesson they taught using it, it won't be perfect for you unless you can connect with it and put your personal stamp on it in some way. Shopping for books is akin to shopping for clothes—if we don't take the time to try them on to see how they fit, they are destined to remain in our closets and on our shelves.

Use precise language. Be precise when you share your thinking. Say what you need to say as clearly and concisely as you can, then move on. Use real language and standard terminology when talking with children; nothing says "inferring" quite like "inferring." Once you've decided on how you'll define a strategy and how you'll format your responses to the reading, keep your language the same. Remember, you're the model. What you say and how you say it becomes what they say and how they say it!

■ ■ ■

When I begin to teach children how to think out loud, I have the same expectations for them as I do for myself. I want their think-alouds to be genuine, their language precise, their responses thoughtful. I start by helping them format their responses. My goal is to give them a framework for thinking, as well as to help them build a common language for talking about books. For example, when children share their connections, I ask them to begin this way: "When I read [or heard] these words . . . it reminded me of . . ." or "When I saw the picture of . . . it made me think about. . . ."

Asking children to recall the words or point out the picture keeps their connection text based and gives the rest of us a point of reference as we listen and learn from their thinking. If a child says only, "My neighbor brings us flowers," I might say, "What were the words in the story that made you think about your neighbor?" If the child doesn't know, I'll reread the page and ask him to listen carefully. When he identifies the appropriate section I say, "So when you heard the words about the lady growing and sharing flowers with her neighbors, it reminded you of your neighbor who shares his huge sunflowers with you? Is that right? Now you try it!"

When the children and I share our connections (or mental images, inferences, questions, and so on) to enhance understanding and construct meaning, I call it *thinking through the text together* (Anderson et al. 1992). This early phase of "having at it" is essential both now and throughout the year, because here readers have opportunities for activating, building, changing, and revising their schema as they engage in conversation with their peers and their teacher.

Early in the year, thinking through text together helps children become aware of what's going on inside their heads as I read, learn how to articulate their thinking for themselves and others, and think aloud about their connections or mental images. Later, as read-alouds and children's thinking grow in sophistication, thinking through text together also allows real opportunities for constructing meaning, reflection, and insight.

Asking children to get eye-to-eye and knee-to-knee is another early way to have at it, and allows more voices to be heard. When I say, "One, two, three, eye-to-eye and knee-to-knee," children turn to someone sitting close to them and think out loud about something I ask them to discuss from the read-aloud or mini-lesson. They might share connections, predict outcomes and explain their reasons for the prediction, create a definition for a strategy, or even develop a plan for resolving an issue on the playground—anything that gives them practice thinking out loud about their thinking. This format is also useful when many children want to share, or when you want to encourage children who are shy or reluctant to share in the large group.

■ ■ ■

Once children understand what they're being asked to do, you'll begin to see a change in how they respond to the read-alouds. But what do we do with all this great thinking? How can we "hold thinking"—make it both permanent and visible?

Recording children's talk in my notebook and creating large (24-by-36-inch) charts based on what they have to say is one way to make thinking permanent and trace our work together. I can't possibly chart everything (though I am known as the "chart lady" in some circles), but I do create "anchor charts" after lessons from which I want children to remember a specific strategy or concept. I write a note of explanation at the top of the chart and note snippets of conversation, individual comments, and statements that reflect our work together.

Anchor charts make our thinking permanent and visible, and so allow us to make connections from one strategy to another, clarify a point, build on earlier learning, and simply remember a specific lesson.

The First Schema Lesson

"Girls and boys, you know how we've been learning about what good readers do when they come to a word they don't know? Well, today we are going to begin learning about what good readers do to better understand and have fun with their reading. Do you know that great readers think and read at the same time? You do? That's so smart! Teachers know that, too, and we've learned that one of the most important things readers do when they read is to make connections from what they already know to information in the text.

"Thinking about what you already know is called *using your schema,* or using your background knowledge. Schema is all the stuff that's already inside your head, like places you've been, things you've done, books you've read—all the experiences you've had that make up who you are and what you know and believe to be true. When you use your schema, it helps you use what you know to better understand and interact with the text."

I look out at Whit and notice his socks still require attention. Kenta's hands are outside his Bronco shirt, but now they're picking rocks out of the soles of his orange and blue Nikes, making little piles. Bret's braiding appears to be nearing completion.

"There are many ways readers use schema, but today we are going to talk about just one way: using schema to make connections from our reading, or the text, to ourselves. We'll call these *text-to-self connections.* When you make connections when you read, it's kind of like having a conversation going on in your head."

Twenty-seven blank faces stare up at me. Two parents have joined us; make that twenty-nine. I forge ahead. "Let me show you what I mean. I'm going to read a story to you; its title is *The Relatives Came* by Cynthia Rylant. I'll read for a while, then I'll stop and think out loud to show you how I use my schema, or what I already know, to make connections from my life to the story. I'm going to let you know what's going on inside my head while I'm reading the story out loud to you."

To avoid confusion between reading and thinking, I tell them, "When I'm holding the book up like this, I'll be reading. When the book is down on my lap like this, I'll be thinking out loud. Are you ready?"

Text-to-Self Connections

"This page makes me laugh. You see right here, where I read to you, 'It was different, going to sleep with all that new breathing in the house'? I understand exactly what Cynthia Rylant meant. That's because *at the same time I was reading,* I was making a connection to when I was a little girl, remembering how my family and all my cousins and aunts and uncles would visit my grandparents in their farmhouse on old Route 92 near Oskaloosa, Iowa.

"Sometimes it was so hot and sticky at night that we'd all pile down to the living room—just like in this picture—because it was the only air-conditioned place in the house. We'd sleep together on the black carpet with the pink and red roses intertwined, listening to Aunt Rosie's scary Melvin stories and dreaming of Shetland pony rides, the midway at the state fair, and Grandma's gingerbread boy or girl pancakes."

As soon as I've shared my connection to the text, I say, "Did you notice how much fun I was having just thinking about being with my cousins and sleeping downstairs on those hot Iowa nights? I'll probably always remember *The Relatives Came* because of all the connections I make while I'm reading it."

When I get to the page where the relatives are heading back to Virginia and everyone is waving good-bye, I read it, then put the book in my lap.

"I love this part. When I saw the picture of the people standing in their pajamas and waving the relatives off in the dark, right away I began to think about a good-bye game my grandma and I used to play. It was called 'Kissed You Last.' When we'd get up so early in the morning to drive back to Colorado, my grandma and I would always see who would get to kiss the other one last. I would always win, because I kept blowing kisses all the way down the lane and onto the highway! I loved playing that game. Do you see how using my schema helped me understand just how the people in the book feel?"

As the story ends, I notice I have everyone's attention. The two parents are smiling. Encouraged, I can't wait to talk about what the children are thinking. "So what did you notice?" I ask. Only Cory raises his hand. "Can we go read now?" he asks. "Oh, brother," I'm thinking, but I say with a smile, "Absolutely. Happy reading, everyone!"

Over the next two weeks there will be similar lessons. I think aloud on consecutive days—Julie Brinkloe's *Fireflies* and Gloria Houston's *My Great-Aunt Arizona* are two favorites. By this time children are usually itching to have their say, and while I continue to model my connections, I encourage them to share theirs, too. This is when we begin thinking through the text together and getting eye-to-eye and knee-to-knee. *Koala Lou* by Mem Fox, *The Snowy Day* by Ezra Jack Keats, and *Chrysanthemum* by Kevin Henkes never fail to engage kids and get them connecting.

At this point I begin scripting and charting their responses. Kids love to see their connections (and their name) in print, and it shows them how much I value what they have to say. Charting holds thinking—it makes our thinking public and permanent, and traces our work together.

Making Meaningful Connections

When I first began teaching children about using their schema to help them make connections to text, they connected to everything! I remember children waving their hands wildly, making the dreaded "Uunh! Uunh! Uunh!" sound, barely able to contain themselves. When I'd call on them, they might say something like, "I have a connection! You know the author of the book?" And I'd say, "You mean Eve Bunting?" "Yeah. Well my cousin's name is Eve." "Really?" I'd say, and on we'd go. And there'd be other comments, like, "I have a red dress, too," or, in response to a picture of a tiny bird in the upper corner of an illustration, "I once had a bird." Then another child would say, "You had a bird? I have a bird right now! His name is Sal." And then, "Sal? That's a girl's name!" Giggles ensue. By this time, neither Eve Bunting nor I could get the kids back.

It's not that I now get only brilliant, meaningful connections from children—every year someone knows an Eve or has a red dress, too, or even once had a bird. But I've learned it's up to me to teach through these kinds of connections. Now I know it's up to me to gently redirect the children's tangential responses right away before they become the norm.

Thinking Through Text Together:
An Anchor Chart in the Making

I begin a mini-lesson several days later this way: "You know how we've been talking about the difference between connections that help us with our reading and the ones that don't? I have an idea that might help us. Today when I'm reading aloud to you, I'm going to record your connections in my notebook, and after school I'll write them on a chart so you can see them. Tomorrow we'll talk about them and figure out which kinds of connections help us most."

After school I transfer all the children's responses to a chart, which reads as follows:

> We have been learning that expert readers make connections from the text to themselves to better understand their reading. When we read *Hazel's Amazing Mother* by Rosemary Wells, we made these text-to-self-connections:
>
> - I helped the mailman once.
> - I have a calico cat.
> - I once got lost in the mall and I was so scared!
> - My grandma made me a doll.
> - I have new shoes, too.
> - My neighbor's name is Hazel.
> - Once my sister was playing and the big kids took her ball. My dad came out and told them to go home.
> - Belle's story about her mom and "the power of love."

The next day we decide to put a "1" next to each response that helped us with the text and a "2" next to responses that didn't help us. I tell the children that as I reread the story, they should think about the connections we made yesterday and try to figure out which ones help us understand the story best.

"Let's look at the first one," I say when I finish reading. "'I helped the mailman once.' Does that help us learn more about the story?" A chorus of no's. (I put a 2 there.)

"And this one: 'I have a calico cat.' Do you think that connection will help us?" More no's. (Another 2.)

"What about this? 'I once got lost in the mall and I was so scared!' Does this one help us?" Olivia answers, "It could help. Put a 1 there." I think to myself, "A 1? What's meaningful about the mall?" But I say, "Keep talking, Olivia. Tell us why you think there should be a 1 there."

"Well, if you had really ever been lost in the mall, it would help you understand how Hazel felt when she got lost. You would get it." Wow, I think, she's right! And I wonder: How many times have I missed opportunities like this one? How many times have I not pursued a child's thinking simply because it didn't fit with mine?

I think, "Thank you, Olivia!" but I say, "What are the rest of you thinking? Put a thumb up if you agree with Olivia." Twenty-six thumbs come up, and though I understand they all don't get it, I know that some of them learned something from Olivia just now, and there will be more opportunities just like this one.

We go on down the chart, marking 1's and 2's as we go. When we finish, I ask, "What can we learn from all this great thinking we just did?"

Taylor, who up to now has just been listening, says, "Well, I think that when something is only on one page, and you make a connection to it, and then it just gets, umm, well, it just kinda gets swept out of the story, that connection isn't going to help you much."

Justin looks at Taylor and says, "Yeah, 'cause it's not so much about the story—it's not a very big connection." "Yeah," Taylor nods. "A tiny little connection isn't going to help you much."

"Taylor and Justin," I say, "I loved the way you two just had a conversation, and I think I see what you mean. Boys and girls, how do you think we might write that on our chart?"

Kendal answers, "How 'bout if we connect to a *word*, like *mailman* or *cat* or *soccer ball*, that doesn't really help us, but if we connect to a bigger thing, like if it's on almost all the pages and it's what the book is really about, like an idea or something, then it can help you."

"Let's see if I've got it," I say. "Do you mean that if we make a connection to a word, like *mailman,* or maybe someone's *name,* it probably won't be as helpful as connecting to something the book keeps coming back to, like a big idea? Taylor, Justin, Kendal, everybody, do we have it?" Heads nod, and I record it on the *Hazel* chart.

"My husband was right," I think. "It's not even November, and already I can't believe how smart they are!"

Releasing Responsibility: Small-Group Work

Once I know what I want children to do in small groups, I need to think through each lesson carefully. What words will I use to explain the lesson and its procedures clearly? What language will best convey my thinking and serve as a model for theirs? What must I do to ensure that when their work together begins, the tone of the classroom is not broken by children who don't know what to do, where to go, or what to do when they're finished?

I'm explicit. I let children in on what we'll be doing and why, what it will look like, and my expectations for their work together.

It's 10 A.M., and children are sprawled every which way on the worn, warehouse-issue carpet. They are in groups of threes and fours, clustered around three-foot-square pieces of white butcher paper. Arms and legs, markers and crayons, are everywhere.

Before reading aloud *Ira Sleeps Over* by Bernard Waber, I tell the children, "Today while I'm reading, I want you to keep your connections *inside* your heads." I explain that once the story is over, they will go to one of the big pieces of paper on the floor (one child to a side, four to a group), talk together about their connections to the story, and record their most important one using pictures, words, or both. There is a copy of the book for each group (this isn't essential, but the multiple copies do help focus and support young readers).

As the children work in their groups, I talk with a few, but mostly I listen. Now, and during share time, I do some informal assessment. I want to know things like

- Are children making real connections to the story?
- Do they understand how these connections help them?
- What kind of language do they use when they talk to each other in small groups?

I listen in on Whit, Ana, Maggie, and Cory. They are busy arranging the paper just so, deciding who will sit where, and arguing about where the exact middle of the paper is so they can place the markers there. Whit turns his back to the group and at least begins to flip through the book, but the conversation for Maggie, Cory, and Ana turns to crayons.

I'm groaning inside. Where's that great talk I know they're capable of? But I resist getting in the middle of it. I glance around the room to see how the other groups are doing and decide to stay where I am. I listen in again. Ana is talking. "Remember the part of the story when he wanted his teddy bear but it was at home? Well, that part reminded me of when I didn't have my teddy bear, and I really wanted it. Remember when everyone had lice? My mom made me put all my stuffed animals in a big trash bag and I couldn't sleep with anything for a whole week! It was terrible. That's what I'm going to write about. Then I'll make a big trash bag right here . . ."

I start itching again (how long do lice live, anyway?), but Cory, Maggie, and Whit are writing and drawing. Relieved, I remember that it often takes adults a while to get focused—why should it be any different for children? I check in with the other groups and notice Jake has drawn a picture of a little boy in a bed (Jake) and a little boy in the doorway waving good-bye (Keenan). He writes, "The first time I went to Keenan's house for a sleep-over, I wasn't homesick. But when he came to my house, he was. He's coming again, and I hope he makes it." Many children have drawn pictures of teddy bears, best friends, and beds.

About thirty minutes later, the big papers are stacked in the middle of our meeting area, the children seated in a large circle around them. "Let's have the group whose paper is on top tell us about their connections first," I tell them. "Sit on the side of the paper that shows your work."

As the small groups share, I discover that many children are making connections to the story and are able to share them with others. I recognize that fewer are able to think aloud about how making connections helps them as readers, and most of those who do use my words ("It helps me understand how Ira feels"). I remind myself (again) that children can use a strategy without fully understanding it and that they will gradually gain control of it through continued modeling and guided practice.

Text-to-Text Connections

When most children are able to make meaningful text-to-self connections—primarily in response to read-alouds and small-group work, but sometimes also in their own reading—I begin to model and think aloud about how and why readers use their schema to make connections from one text to another. It's tempting at this point to forgo thinking aloud to show kids how. I used to assume that once children had become successful at making text-to-self connections, the rest would come naturally. Not anymore! Now, when I think about gradually releasing responsibility, I realize that children—and teachers, too—move in and out of all phases (thinking aloud, having at it, and letting go) several times during the teaching of each strategy. Whenever I teach something new, I've learned to take the time to be explicit and show children how.

Amazing Grace by Mary Hoffman and Tomie dePaola's *Oliver Button Is a Sissy* are a good pair of books to read aloud and demonstrate how making text-to-text connections can help readers construct meaning and enhance understanding. I read *Oliver Button* first, and we talk through the text together, making connections about teasing, bullies, talent shows, and moms and dads. The next day I read *Amazing Grace.* By way of introduction, I tell the children that they're getting so good at making text-to-self connections, I want to teach them how readers make other kinds of connections, too. "Let me show you what I mean . . ."

When we get to the part where Raj tells Grace she can't be Peter Pan because she isn't a boy and Natalie whispers that Grace can't be Peter Pan because she's black, I stop reading, put the book in my lap, and think aloud.

"You know, when I read these last two pages, where Raj told Grace she couldn't be Peter Pan because she isn't a boy and Natalie said she couldn't because Peter Pan isn't black, it reminded me of the book *Oliver Button Is a Sissy.* Do you remember the part where all the boys are making fun of him because he loves to dance? Look—see right here? I'm thinking of Oliver Button at the same time I'm reading about Amazing Grace, and I'm thinking they're alike in some ways. When it said that Grace keeps her hand up to be Peter Pan, even when Natalie and Raj didn't think she could be, I remembered that Oliver Button didn't give up, either, just because those boys were teasing him.

"When readers do what I just did—when they make a connection from a book that they're reading to one they've read before—that's called making a *text-to-text connection.* Making text-to-text connections, or connections from one book to another book, can help you understand the new story and make predictions about what may happen based on what you know from the other story. Let's keep reading and see what happens next."

When we get to the part where the class meets for auditions, I put the book down again. "Right now, I'm predicting Grace is going to be Peter Pan in the play. You know why I'm thinking that? Remember my earlier connections to Oliver Button, and how he practiced and practiced, just like Grace did? And even though he didn't win first prize in the talent show, things worked out for him and the boys didn't tease him anymore? I think it might be the same for Grace, too. I think she'll be chosen to play Peter Pan in the school play, and I predict that Natalie and Raj are going to realize that what they said to her was wrong and start being nicer to her. What do you think?"

The class's prediction is unanimous, and is later confirmed. At the end of the story, when I ask the kids what they noticed as I was making text-to-text connections, Whit says, "I saw you doing lots of things, like stopping to think, making predictions, and making connections to Oliver Button." "Wow," I think, as I record his words. "What a difference a couple of weeks makes!" But I say, "Good noticing, Whit! Anyone else?"

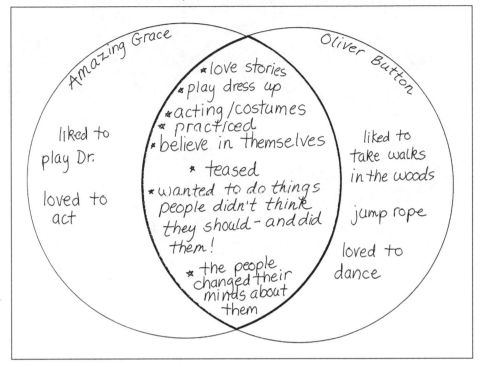

Text-to-text connections go beyond comparing characters, of course; but for early readers, it's the perfect place to begin. Creating Venn diagrams to compare characters or other features in pairs of books can show children in a very visual way how text-to-text connections help the reader make predictions and enhance understanding. (Figure 5.1 shows my charting of connections between *Oliver Button* and *Amazing Grace;* Figure 5.2 shows Emily's own Venn diagram of connections between *Now One Foot, Now the Other* by Tomie dePaola and *The Two of Them* by Aliki. You'll find that children also love to compare different versions of the same story, particularly fairy tales; and stories or other texts by the same author.

Schema Throughout the Year

Schema doesn't end with text-to-self and text-to-text connections. Throughout the year I teach children to use and develop their schema for making text-to-world connections and exploring individual authors, partic-

FIGURE 5.2 Emily's connections between *Now One Foot, Now the Other* by Tomie dePaola and *The Two of Them* by Aliki

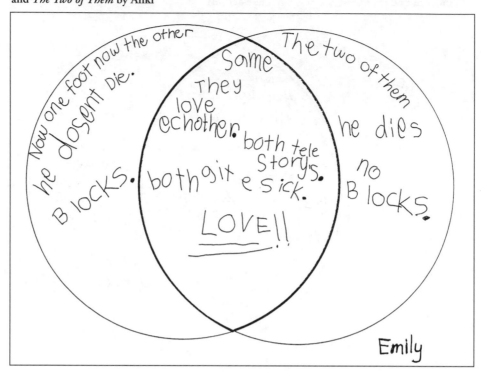

ular types of text, text features and characteristics, and topics of interest to the children.

Text-to-World Connections

I teach children about making text-to-world connections by listening and paying attention to what they have to say and being aware of what's going on in the world. I used to think children as young as six, seven, and eight needn't wrestle with real-world issues such as war, homelessness, poverty, and prejudice. But when it's the buzz on the playground and in the lunchroom, when it's blaring from radios, televisions, and newspapers, it's time to talk.

I've learned that children love to grapple with complex social and moral issues, and they often have clearer heads than some grown-ups I know! Sometimes I search for just the right book to help me launch the discussion; other times a read-aloud will spark a discussion about something I hadn't planned. Memorable text-to-world connections include

■ Kevan's connection between *Smoky Night* by Eve Bunting and the mini-riots the night the Broncos won the Super Bowl.

- Ailey's connection between *I Have a Dream* by Mike Francen and a swastika that was burned onto our school's playing field.
- Max's connection between *Miss Maggie* by Cynthia Rylant and his aunt who has Alzheimer's disease.
- Taylor and Keenan's connection between *How Many Days to America?* by Eve Bunting and the war in Kosovo.
- Lilli's connection between *Lifetimes* by Bryan Mellonie and Robert Ingpen and the rampage at Columbine High School.
- Edward's connection between a newspaper article about fighting in the Balkans and gang activity in his neighborhood.
- Children's connections between a magazine article about the September 11 tragedy in New York City and our own class "Promise to Each Other."

Building Schema for Authors, Types of Text, and Text Elements

Because most early readers have limited schema for individual authors, types of text, and text features and characteristics, I work throughout the year to build schema in these areas. Teaching children to activate what they know when they

- encounter a book by a familiar author
- select a picture book, songbook, or early reader
- read poetry, narrative, or expository text

helps them know what to expect and how best to go about reading and making sense of a particular text. I have three charts displayed and we add to them whenever we become familiar with an author, learn about a different type of text, or work with characteristics and features that are unique to poetry, narrative, or expository text.

Topic Study: Activating, Building, and Revising Schema

Whenever we begin a new topic of study, I begin by asking, "So what's our schema for this? What do we know about —?" To help children activate what they already know I sometimes liken the schema to opening mental files in their heads. I tell them that sometimes we have to stop and think about what we already know; we have to search our brains for that mental file, open it, and make connections between what we know and the new information. I show the children some of my paper files, as well as those I've created on the classroom computer. I model how I make new files, add information to existing files, and revise and delete information.

"The files in your brain are a lot like these files," I tell them. "You can work with them the same way. Let's try it. Remember yesterday when Maggie asked the question, 'Why do leaves change color?' Open your mental files right now—what information do you already have in your head that would help answer her question?" I record each response on a 5-by-7-inch sheet of paper and place the sheet in a paper file labeled "Why do leaves change color?"

The next day I read aloud a text on the subject and as we encounter new information, I write it down and add it to the file created the day before. When we finish, we open the file and look closely at our thinking and learning. We determine what information should be kept in the file and what information should be crossed out or deleted. Figure 5.3 shows a chart that records this process.

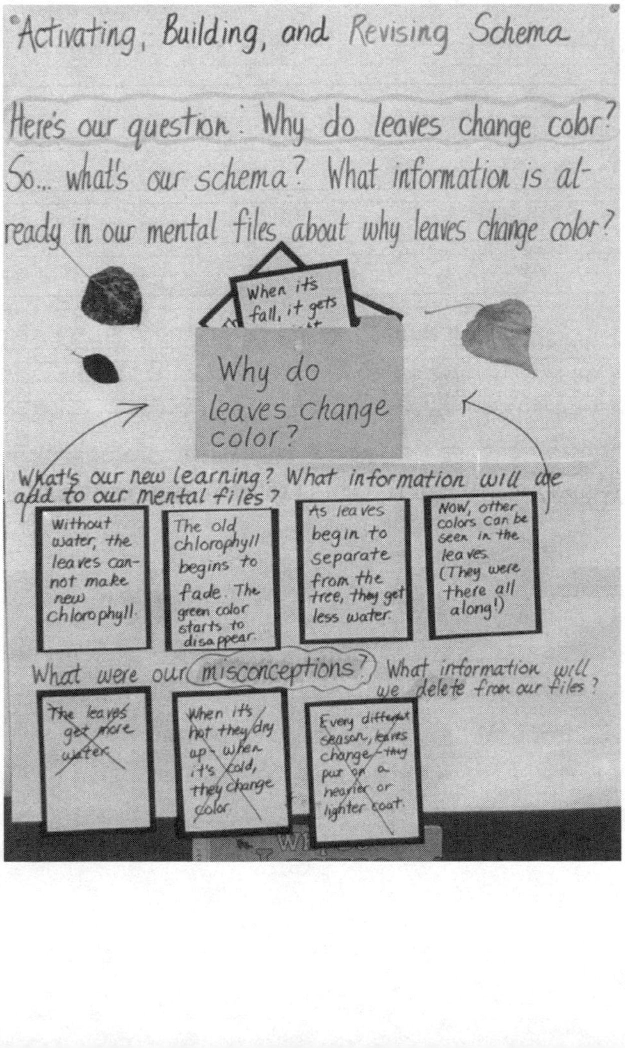

FIGURE 5.3 A schema chart

■ Evidence of Understanding and Independence

Nicole
I Know A Lady
Connections

On are bloc thar lives a lady
who livs alon. Evry day she's
aot side Planting flours. She smiols
a warm and tentle smiol. When
she Smiols I thike she
loves me.

Nicole's connection to *I Know a Lady* by Charlotte Zolotow

"When you use schema, it's like adding things together. Say you see leaves falling. You think in your head, 'Oh, it's fall now!' It's kind of like your old schema comes out of your head and grabs the new schema and pulls it back inside your head."
Christopher

"Schema is what you know; it's your thinking."
Madi

"When you change your thinking about something, you change your schema."
Devon

"Everything you hear and see and feel, everyplace you go and everything you do, puts more schema into your head."
Grant

Name Nina
Date 12-7-00

Roxaboxen- Thinking About Connections

When I heard the part about	it reminded me of
The KidS PLAying War	My GranPPa GOt hurt in The War.

Nina's connection to _Roxaboxen_ by Alice McLerran

When it said if I've Told You once I've Told You a Million time's No Jumping on the bed I have a coneckshun. When I jump on The Bed—

My dad says if you Tump on the Bed one more Time You will be Tickld untill you criye!!

Abby's connection to _No Jumping on the Bed_ by Tedd Arnold

> I have a
> conekshone.
> Wen I Get
> out of the
> Swiming Pol I
> am Soking
> Wet! I tell
> my Mom I
> am cold

> ME and Mi
> DaD DO
> SOM things
> BI OR
> SLFs.

> But she
> all Redye
> knows I
> am Just
> Going to
> Get Back
> in agan
> and Play.

> X-t   When Hansel
> and Gretel saw the
> Witch I made a
> cunecshun to Bony
> Legs.

(Left column) Emily's connection to *Amelia Bedelia Goes Camping* by Peggy Parish; (upper right) Whit's connection to *Just Me and My Dad* by Mercer Mayer; (lower right) Chris's connection to *Hansel and Gretel*

Schema at a Glance

What's Key for Kids?

- Readers activate their prior knowledge before, during, and after reading.
- Readers use schema to make connections between the text and their lives, between one text and another, and between the text and the world.
- Readers distinguish between connections that are meaningful and relevant and those that aren't.

- Readers build, change, and revise their schema when they encounter new information in the text, engage in conversations with others, and gain personal experience.
- Readers use their schema to enhance understanding.

(Adapted from Keene and PEBC)

Tried and True Texts for Schema

Fireflies by Julie Brinkloe
Hazel's Amazing Mother by Rosemary Wells
I Know a Lady by Charlotte Zolotow
Ira Sleeps Over by Bernard Waber
Koala Lou by Mem Fox
My Great-Aunt Arizona by Gloria Houston
Now One Foot, Now the Other by Tomie dePaola
Oliver Button Is a Sissy by Tomie dePaola
The Relatives Came by Cynthia Rylant
Roxaboxen by Alice McLerran
The Snowy Day by Ezra Jack Keats
The Two of Them by Aliki

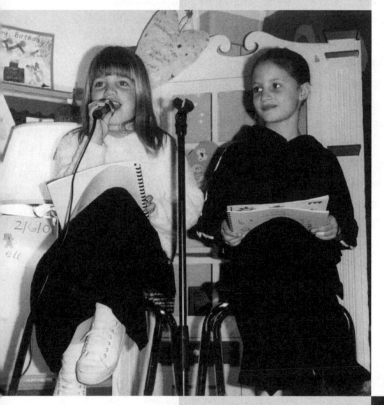

Madison and Camille offer greetings and poems during Coffeehouse Poetry Day.

6

Creating Mental Images

Matthew works hard to create mental images as he listens to *My Father's Dragon* by Ruth Stiles Gannet.

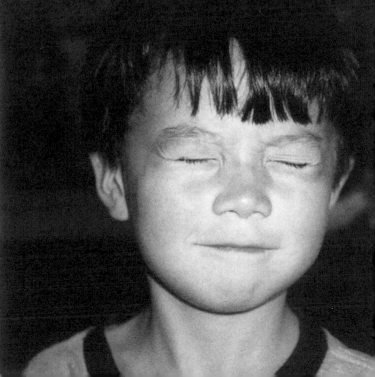

The muted trumpet of Miles Davis plays on the CD player, floating among the voices in the crowded classroom. Hot chocolate simmers in the PTA's relic of a coffeepot; a mountain of miniature marshmallows fills a bowl nearby. Long rolls of deep blue paper decorated with construction paper stars, coffee cups, planets, flowers, hearts, and crescent moons cover the windows and darken the room. Table lamps and tiny white lights draped from the ceiling provide the only light.

Freshly scrubbed tables are rearranged into cozy groups of two. Handmade flowers in tiny clay pots, poetry books, bowls of pretzels, and small containers of words from magnetic poetry kits have replaced crayons, markers, scissors, sticky notes, pencils, and glue.

Parents and children sit together, munching pretzels and sipping steamy hot chocolate in mugs brought from home, reading poetry by the likes of Eloise Greenfield, Maya Angelou, Aileen Fisher, Jane Yolen, Valerie Worth, and Georgia Heard. But the poems receiving the most enthusiastic reviews? They're the ones written by the children themselves, published and bound into books with enough copies for everyone.

Black is the clothing color of choice; berets adorn the heads of the truly hip. Starbucks, you say? No way! We've transported ourselves back to the 1960s (ancient history to everyone in the room but me) and it's Coffeehouse Poetry Day in Room 104.

It's time to begin. I know because the sixth child has just asked me when we're going to start, and I see numbers seven and eight approaching. I give Frank a wink and a nod. He walks to the makeshift stage—a table with two chairs taped on top, a red step stool to get there, and a well-used microphone gleaned from an enterprising custodian. He climbs the steps and sings into the microphone, "Everybody listen!" The response is deafening: "Right now!" Startled parents look up, stunned at their children's silence. Finally, they, too, stop talking. This signals Madison to the stage.

Microphone in hand, she begins. "Welcome, parents, children, and friends, to our Coffeehouse Poetry Day. We've been learning how readers and writers create mental images when they read and write. When we read our poems, we want you to see if you can create some mental images, too. Listen and wait for the pictures to come alive in your minds."

Abby begins. "Hi, everyone! I'm Abby and the title of my poem is 'Dolphins.' Dolphins dive / into the ocean. / Flippity flop! / Splishity splash! / Dolphins never stop. / Twisting, twirling / in the shining sunlight, / all day long." One by one, and sometimes in twos, children extend greetings and read their poems into the microphone. I'm at the ready, turning up the volume of Miles's muted trumpet between poems, turning it down as children read.

Icicles
Icicles drip
in the morning light,
and freeze
in the darkness
of the night.
Icicles scream
as if they were talking
to the wind.
   Caroline

Trains
Trains rumble over tracks.
Big black tunnels wait.
Dark metal zooms
through the night.
   Zach

Henry
When I hold my Guinea Pig
Henry
he makes me feel
safe inside.
Warm fur
red eyes
chubby little body.
Henry is my buddy.
   Olivia

The Changes of the World
When winter falls,
it seems like years have passed.
Layers and layers of rock
lay silent
on the stiff, brown ground. I look out
my bedroom window.
It seems like things have changed
in the world,
and people have gotten older.
   Zachary

Hot Tubs
Hot tubs,
steamy bubbles,
powerful jets,
ZOOM like shallow waves
in the ocean.
San Diego hot tubs,
that's where I want to be!
  Griffin

Poppy
I remember my Grandpa.
I used to go everywhere he'd go.
He fixed me really good bacon.
I used to love to sleep next to him.
I really miss my Poppy.
  Cory

Space
In space
stars twinkle
in the darkness of night.
Saturn's rings twirl
and planets swirl
as if they were dancing.
  Emily

Sunday Morning on CBS
Football people
race across the field,
leaping to tackle you
to the green and grassy ground.
  Devon

Leaves
The leaves
tiptoe to the ground
with only a soft, gentle sound.
We hear the leaves go
crinkle, crackle,

crunch, crunch
under our feet.
We rake them into a mountain
of red, orange,
yellow, brown and purple.
The leaves
tiptoe to the ground
with only a soft, gentle sound.
　　Madison and Camille

When you read about Coffeehouse Poetry Day just now, did you find yourself creating images in your head? Maybe you visualized a classroom (yours?) with tiny white lights overhead, or pictured twenty-seven children and their parents dressed in black. Maybe you caught a whiff of the hot chocolate and heard the notes of a trumpet, or the children's boisterous "Right now!" And just maybe you noticed a lump in your throat when you read Cory's poem about his Poppy.

When readers create mental images, they engage with text in ways that make it personal and memorable to them alone. Anchored in prior knowledge, images come from the emotions and all five senses, enhancing understanding and immersing the reader in rich detail (Keene and Zimmermann 1997).

In the Beginning: Thinking Aloud

A favorite book for thinking aloud about creating mental images is *Night Sounds, Morning Colors* by Rosemary Wells. The inside flap issues an invitation: "Look. Listen. Open all your senses." Who could resist? Violets laugh and sing in Mama's garden, a father hums "Danny Boy" as he tucks his little boy into bed, a train whistles through the darkness of the night.

"Listen again to the words about the faraway train and its whistle," I say to the children during the read-aloud. "When I read those words, such vivid images, or pictures, come into my mind. I have an image of my mother, brother, and me streaking across the flatlands of Kansas on a train called the *El Capitán*. I see us looking up at the night sky through the skylights above us, my brother and I thinking we could count the stars. I hear the rumble of the wheels on the tracks, and the porters in their fancy red and black outfits talking in whispers outside our compartment.

"Even now I can feel the excitement of going to the dining car for breakfast. I have images of starched white tablecloths, deep red napkins the size of my mother's silk scarves, fragrant fresh flowers in silver vases, and more knives, forks, and spoons at each setting than one little girl could possibly use. And the cinnamon rolls! My image of them fills an entire plate, with yummy white frosting slowly oozing down into little puddles at the bottom.

"Girls and boys, did you notice how creating mental images seemed to make the text come alive for me? It's like I was back on the *El Capitán,* streaking across the countryside, looking up at the stars, sitting down in that fancy dining car, and eating those yummy cinnamon rolls all over again. The page about the train will always be important to me—I'll always remember it—because of my connections to it and the images they create in my mind. Someone else reading the book would have different images, because that person's schema is different. No one else, not even my mother or brother, would remember those train rides the same way I do."

I take a couple of days with the Wells book, sharing one or two pages each day and talking about how the images I create enhance my reading and understanding of the text. On day three, I say to the children, "Lie down, close your eyes, and listen to the words as I read. Pay attention to the images that come alive in your mind. Put your thumb up when an image comes into your head."

They're into it. Flat on the floor, eyes scrunched shut, they wait with anticipation. I read the fish page, and one tiny thumb after another shoots up, vying for attention. Not only do they see fish weaving in and out of pagodas, as in the book, but they become fish right before my eyes! Big fish with bulging eyes, puckered lips, and swishing tails squirm (swim?) around the meeting area.

A fish named Frank stops midstream and says, "Wait a minute, guys. What's a pagoda?" And before I know it, four children try to fashion one with their bodies. Emily says, "Look, Frank, see? It's one of those tall Chinese-like houses—you know, the ones with the curvy roofs? I have one in my fish tank, and the fish really do swim in and out of the windows and the doors. Swim through this door right here!" Frank swishes right through.

I think, "Well, Debbie, this isn't quite what you'd expected, but what's happening is a good thing, right? Uh . . . right." I'm grateful it wasn't a page full of tigers.

The page with the birthday cake sends thumbs flying once again. They can see that birthday cake!

"How many candles are on your cake?" I ask.

"Seven! And they're burning hot and bright! Ouch! I just touched one!"

"My cake has just one candle, but it's a big red number three right in the middle. It's my baby brother's cake."

"The cake in my head is big and round and it has a soccer player on it. There are words. Let's see . . . they say [eyes closing tight]—oh! I see them now!—they say 'Happy Birthday, Paige' and 'You're Number One!'"

Next I ask, "What kind of cake is in your image?"

"Chocolate!"

"No! Mine's white with lemon filling, my favorite!"

"Wait! Listen to this! I see an angel food cake with white frosting and pink and red hearts all over it, and seven purple candles and it tastes delicious!"

"Oohs" and "aahs" and "Are we going to have snack?" and "When's lunch?" (two long hours from now) let me know it's time for a change of pace.

"Wow, you created some very vivid mental images—I loved all the details you included," I tell them. "What did you notice about your images of the birthday cakes?"

"Everybody saw a different kind of birthday cake!"

"You're right. They were all different. Why do you suppose that is?"

They chorus as one, "Because our schema is different!"

"Good thinking. I can tell you're going to be really good at this. One last thing. Before you go to read, I'm interested in knowing what you're thinking about creating mental images so far. Any thoughts? Ideas? Questions?"

My pencil and notebook are ready. "It's so much fun!" and "I love making mental images!" and "Can we practice again tomorrow?" are typical responses, but Kenta's thoughts take my breath away. "Well, here's what I'm thinking. I'm thinking mental images are sort of like connections, only a lot bigger. Say a connection is like a kernel of corn. But when you put it in the microwave and it pops up big and hot, now *that's* a mental image. You hear it and see it and smell it and taste it and love it. That's what I'm thinking."

The room is silent; the only sound is that of my pencil furiously writing to catch every word. Madison asks, "Did you get that exactly, Mrs. Miller? We should put it up in the room somewhere." Kenta knows just the spot.

Focusing on just a snippet or two from a picture book or poem allows children time to practice developing an image completely. Asking questions like "How many candles are on your cake?" and "What kind is it?" gives children permission to add details that personalize their images and make them unique. Books such as *Night in the Country* by Cynthia Rylant, *The Salamander Room* by Anne Mazer, *Quiet, Please* by Eve Merriam, *Say*

Something by Mary Stoltz, *The Napping House* by Audrey Wood, *Creatures of Earth, Sea, and Sky* by Georgia Heard, and anything by Joanne Ryder also offer rich snippets of text for thinking aloud, thinking through text together, and getting eye-to-eye and knee-to-knee to talk about mental images.

In addition to picture books, what type of text is best when children begin to become more adept at making mental images on their own? What type of text bridges whole-group work and independence? The answer is poetry. Short, thought-provoking, and full of images, poetry allows even early readers to navigate the text once it's been read aloud several times. I've learned that the best decoders aren't necessarily the most thoughtful readers, nor are the most thoughtful readers necessarily the best decoders. Asking children to read and respond to the same text creates additional opportunities for children with different strengths to listen and learn from each other.

Anchor Lessons

The lessons that follow show how I use a given text to deepen children's understanding of the strategy of making mental images. Using poetry and picture books, children practice creating and adapting images in their minds, and make them concrete through artistic, dramatic, and written responses. Children explore how

- images are created from readers' schema and words in the text
- readers create images to form unique interpretations, clarify thinking, draw conclusions, and enhance understanding
- readers' images are influenced by the shared images of others
- images are fluid; readers adapt them to incorporate new information as they read
- evoking vivid mental images helps readers create vivid images in their writing.

Images are created from readers' schema and words in the text (artistic response)

I make ten or so copies of three or four poems I know children will love—those written by children from previous years are perfect. I think about the content of the poems I choose. Do children have enough schema for the topic? Is the text clear? Do the poems lend themselves to unique interpretations?

I read each poem aloud several times, asking children to "listen carefully and think about which poem creates the most vivid mental images for you." Next I say, "Take a copy of the poem you've chosen and a piece of drawing paper, and find a place you can work well. Read the poem to yourself a couple of times, then capture the image that's in your head as best you can onto paper. Take about ten minutes, then we'll share our work."

When children gather to share, I ask those who have chosen the same poem to sit together, share their images, and talk about what they notice. After the small groups have shared, I ask children to tell the large group what they've learned. Their words may not change ("Our pictures/images are different because our schema is different"), but the experience of this kind of activity helps children anchor their words and give them meaning. (Figure 6.1 shows some responses as displayed in a classroom.)

Readers create images to form unique interpretations, clarify thinking, draw conclusions, and enhance understanding (dramatic response)

While the concepts above are inherent in all the lessons described in this chapter, dramatizing short pieces of text is another way to engage and teach

FIGURE 6.1 One class's mental images

young readers about mental images, as I learned from the fish with the puckered lips in the *Night Sounds, Morning Colors* experience.

I ask children to get together in groups of three or four and find a place where there is enough space for them to work together comfortably. I tell them, "Close your eyes and listen carefully to the poem I'm about to read. Pay special attention to the words in the poem and your schema to create vivid, detailed images."

I read the poem aloud three or four times and ask children to think aloud in their groups about the images they've created. Next I say, "Put your thinking together to create a dramatic interpretation of the poem. Think about things like:

- What about the poem does your group think is most important?
- How will you show that?
- How can everyone be included?"

Books like Martha Robinson's *The Zoo at Night* are good choices for this type of dramatization and interpretation—koalas munch, spider monkeys frolic, the hippo floats, and the giant tortoise looks about to see that all is right with the night. (There are some tiger cubs, but they're peacefully cuddling next to their sleeping mother.)

Later, I ask children to share their dramatic interpretations. I ask each group to talk about why they chose to dramatize the poem the way they did, focusing on how each group chose to interpret the poem in a different way, based on their images and what they believed to be most important.

Children also love to choose their own poems or short pieces of text to dramatize and present to the group. Sometimes the audience tries to guess what the poem is about; other times one or two children will read the poem while others in the group act out their images. Later, when we learn how readers use dramatic responses to figure out a tricky word (like *pagoda*) or understand a puzzling piece of text, children will have had practice with this type of response.

Readers' images are influenced by the shared images of others (artistic response)

I choose Georgia Heard's poem "Ducks on a Winter Night" because I know it's a poem my children have some schema for, yet is sophisticated enough to require thoughtful interpretation. It reads:

Reading with Meaning

Ducks asleep
on the banks of the pond
tuck their bills
into feathery quills,
making their own beds
to keep warm in.

I write the poem on chart paper, and the children and I read it together three or four times. We don't talk much about images or meaning; I ask children to go to their seats and draw the images they've created from the poem independently. Next, I ask them to share their images with the person sitting next to them and talk about not only their images, but also the bit of text that inspired that particular image.

When they finish, I say, "Let's read the poem again. As we read, pay attention to your images this time through. After learning about your partner's image and rereading the text, would you change the image you've drawn in any way? Did your partner's image change your understanding of the poem? Did rereading the text change the way you picture it?" After the children have listened to the poem again, I say, "Go to the other side of your paper and draw your image as you see it now."

At their tables, the children share their work. This was a great help for Nicole. She had originally thought the quills referred to in the poem were porcupine quills; after a conversation with her partner, Abby, she had a much better understanding of the poem (see page 89).

Images are fluid; readers adapt them to incorporate new information as they read (artistic response)

Up until now, most lessons I've described have focused on creating detailed images in response to a poem or a short piece of text. These types of images aren't the kind that change much once they've been created. But with Jane Yolen's book *Greyling*, I show children how readers' mental images can be fluid, that they can change to incorporate new information.

Greyling is the story of a fisherman and his wife who live in a moss-covered hut by the sea, longing for nothing more than a child of their own. One day the fisherman finds a small grey seal stranded on a sandbar. But this is no regular seal. . . .

The first day, without showing children the pictures, I read aloud the first half of the book, quickly sketching some of my most vivid images on sticky notes and thinking aloud about how they change as I continue to read and learn more about the story. When I finish, I place them on the dry-erase board.

"Let's take another look at my images," I say. "Do you see how they changed as I kept reading? Here I have an image of a seal in the fisherman's arms, and in this sketch my image of the seal has changed into a little boy. As I continue to read, the images in my head continue to change, too. Do you see?"

"Is it kind of like a movie going on inside your head?" Madison asks. I tell her it's exactly like that. "Tomorrow," I tell the children, "I'll read the rest of the story and you'll have a chance to see what it's like to have a movie going on inside your head, and do some sketching, too."

The next day, the children bring a clipboard and a pencil to the meeting area. I give them a record sheet divided into fourths and headed "Adapting mental images during reading." I reread the first half of the book, showing children the pictures this time through. When we get to where we left off the day before, I say, "Now I'm going to read you the rest of the story. I'm not going to show you the pictures right now; I want you to listen to the words and keep track of how the images in your mind change as I continue to read. I'll read a while, then stop, giving you time to sketch your images. When we finish, we'll take a look to see how you've adapted your images to include new information in the text. Are you ready?"

Figure 6.2 shows one child's response to this exercise.

Evoking vivid mental images helps readers create vivid images in their writing (artistic/written response)

A wonderful consequence of teaching mental images in reading is the effect it has on children's writing. I learned this the day I asked children to draw their images as they listened to a nature CD called *Mountain Streams.* The peaceful sounds filled every corner of the room, and the rich details in the children's drawings caught me by surprise. Orange and pink sunsets, rushing waterfalls, meandering streams, and black-sky thunderstorms covered their sheets of paper.

Just as I'm about to ask children to come up front to share their images, Kenta skips over and whispers in my ear, "My table thinks we should *write* about our mental images, too. Can we? Please?" I tell him it's a brilliant idea and ask him to make an announcement to find out what the rest of the class thinks. They're with him! (And to think I almost missed the boat on this one. . . .)

Children who couldn't seem to get past writing about loving Mom, Dad, brothers, sisters, grandmas, grandpas, dogs, cats, me, trips to the park,

FIGURE 6.2 Whitney's changing mental images for *Greyling* by Jane Yolen

and birthday parties at McDonald's are now writing about cool summer breezes, cabins off in the distance, and swooshing waterfalls splashing their faces with tears. Shawnda writes, "The rushing wind rolls across the Rocky Mountain heights. The stream squiggles down the mountain." And Mitchell, whose topic of choice usually has something to do with monsters, writes, "The golden sun sets behind the purple mountains in flashes of pink and red." As more and more children share, I say, "Guys—your writing is unbelievable today! Your images are so clear, and your words—they sound like poetry! Do you hear what I hear?" Their beaming faces and exuberant nods tell me they do. "So what do you think happened? What made the difference today?"

They attribute their brilliance to the peacefulness, to the beautiful sounds that helped them get ideas, and to the images they created in their minds. I attribute their brilliance to all those things, too, but I know there's more to it. They're writing beautifully because the stage has been set for them. They've been creating images in different contexts for three or four weeks now; I've taught them about detail. They've been listening to and reading poems and stories with beautiful language for three or four weeks, too; I've taught them about rich words. And now they're putting all that learning into yet another context: writing. It's probably no surprise we launch into poetry during this study—or that music is now a ritual in our writers' workshop.

■ Evidence of Understanding and Independence

"My Dad always says I'm daydreaming, but that's not the right word. I'm making mental images and connecting them together. I'm not day-dreaming, I tell him, I'm thinking."
Cory

"When my Mom reads me Harry Potter, *it's like I have a paint set inside my brain. And I never run out of paint!"*
Ben

"Yesterday I was ski-ing so fast I just knew I was in for a major wipeout, and then I made a mental image of what I should do. I could see me curving to slow down in my head, and then I just

Name Maggie

Recording Mental Images

My Mom read me Stuart Little

This is my most vivid mental image:

I had a Mental Image Of the Littles looking for Stuart.

Maggie's mental image from *Stuart Little* **by E. B. White**

I haD A mental image in LITTLE BEAR. I smelD leaves.

Sheldon's mental image from *Little Bear* by Else Holmelund Minarik

when I read the words about momas vos I maDe A Booming mental image I can jest here Flossie's mom Calling her.

Olivia's mental image from *Flossie and the Fox* by Patricia McKissack

did it in real life! My feet started curving. It really helped me!"
Andrew

One day I was telling children how I sometimes listen to Bronco games on the radio when I'm driving. I told them about how I create images in my mind as the announcer describes the action on the field and how it makes the game a lot more interesting and memorable for me. At the end of the story, Nina raised her hand. "Mrs. Miller, there's just one thing I don't get. How do you drive with your eyes closed?"

Dear Debbie,
I started reading Whit The Lion, the Witch, and the Wardrobe several nights ago because he had gotten a little sample of a chapter of it from an annotated youth version with Carol in the doctor's office waiting room. We borrowed Thad's paperback copy

and read the first chapter, which he seemed to soak up well. The only illustrations in the book, however, are very small and simple pen-and-ink sketches covering maybe one-fourth of the first page of each chapter. After we finished the first chapter, Whit hungrily thumbed through the pages until he came to the start of each chapter, looked at the sketch, and asked me to read him the name of the chapter so he could try and figure out what was going to happen in the story. Since this was the first chapter book with minimal illustrations I'd ever read to Whit, I apologized for the lack of illustrations and suggested maybe we could look in the library for a version of the book that had more pictures. Whit kind of gave a sigh, and then said in a slightly condescending tone, "No, Dad. Don't you think we can

> I made a mentil imeg When I heard the words, ofen they Went into the woods to gatheer Berries! I Cluod here the Birds singing!

Emily's mental image from *Snow White and Rose Red* retold by Barbara Cooney

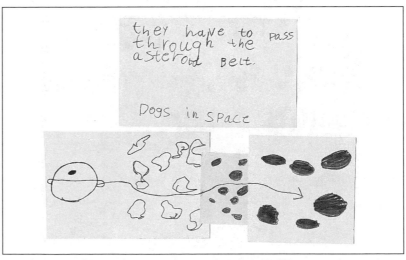

> they have to pass through the asteroid Belt.
>
> Dogs in Space

Brendan's mental image from *Dogs in Space* by Nancy Coffelt

Reading with Meaning

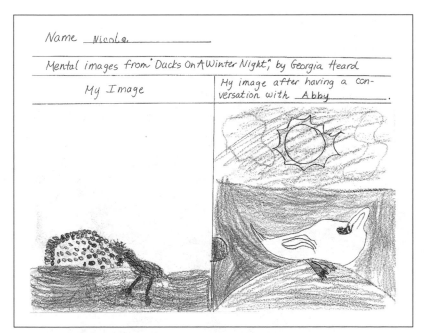

the rabbit was standing in a ray of suhlight.

Colten's mental image from *I Was Walking Down the Road* by Sarah Barchas

Name Nicole

Mental images from "Ducks On A Winter Night", by Georgia Heard

My Image | My image after having a conversation with Abby

Nicole shows how she changed her thinking after conferring with Abby

make mental images as we read the story?"

Thanks for the great year Whit is having!

Hunt Walker

Conferring is often the best window into children's thinking. The things they say and the creative ways they find to apply their learning leave me shaking my head and smiling in amazement, as in the following conferences with Frank and Grace, Daniel, and Kenta.

"Hey, Frank," I say, "how's Little Bear going for you today?" "It's great!" he answers. "And you know what? When I am reading Little Bear, I can just put me right in the story. I'm doing what Little Bear is doing. When I turn the page, it's like someone else is turning the page. See right here? When Little Bear says, 'I'm cold,' I'm cold, too—freezing cold! I'm really shivering, see?" "You do look cold!" I say, as I wonder to myself, "Those couldn't be real goose bumps on his arms, could they?"

At this point Grace, who sits across from Frank, overhears us. "Frank, listen to this," she says. "My mental images are sort of like that, but not exactly. It's like I'm inside the book, like you say, but the book characters don't notice me. I'm part of what's happening, but I'm invisible. Are you invisible, too, or does Little Bear see you?"

"Oh he definitely sees me, and I see him. It's kind of like Little Bear and I are brothers. When Mother Bear made snow pants for Little Bear, she gave them to me, too! And you know what else? I can pop out of one character and into another if I want. Little Bear's image just pulls me in, and I'm not at school anymore. I'm in his life."

▪ ▪ ▪

Abby's mental image from *Ice Stars* by S. A. Kramer

FIGURE 6.3 Kenta's mental image from *Stars and Planets* edited by David Levy

Reading with Meaning

"Hi, Daniel," I say. "Tell me about what you're doing over here in the corner." It looks to me like he's covering entire pages with Post-it notes, but I'm willing to listen.

"I'm covering up all the pictures with Post-its because I want to make my own mental images. These aren't very good. I know that's not what billy goats really look like, and see this troll? Trolls only have one eye and wouldn't wear clothes like that!"

"So you're saying your schema about billy goats and trolls is different from the illustrator's?" I ask him.

Daniel nods yes. "I have lots more schema for billy goats and trolls. See my images?"

"I see what you mean about the one big eye," I say, "and the clothes, too. Your images really are different!"

"Oh," he says, "remember when Ben brought in that picture of Hagrid from Harry Potter *and had a big fit because Hagrid didn't look like Ben's image? It's kind of like the same thing!"*

Kenta wildly motions to me across the room, jumping in and out of his seat. "Look at this!" he says as he points to a picture in the book Stars and Planets *edited by David Levy, a small diagram illustrating how Earth's seasons change. "I really get what you mean about making mental images now! I kept looking at this picture and I didn't get it at all. But then I saw these arrows, and I made it move in my mind! The earth is turning around the sun, and I can see leaves for fall, and snow coming in the winter, and beautiful-smelling flowers in spring, and the hot sun in summer, with people in shorts, all happy and stuff. Here's my mental image of it! See how the sun hits different parts of the earth at different times of the year?" (Figure 6.3 shows Kenta's drawing.)*

Mental Images at a Glance

What's Key for Kids?

- Proficient readers create mental images during and after reading. These images come from all five senses and the emotions and are anchored in the reader's prior knowledge.
- Proficient readers understand how creating images enhances comprehension.
- Proficient readers use images to draw conclusions, create unique interpretations of the text, recall details significant to the text, and recall a text after it has been read.

- Images from reading frequently become part of the reader's writing.
- Readers use images to immerse themselves in rich detail as they read. The detail gives depth and dimension to the reading, engaging the reader more deeply and making the text more memorable.
- Readers adapt their images in response to the shared images of other readers.
- Readers adapt their images as they continue to read. Images are revised to incorporate new information in the text and new interpretations as developed by the reader.
- Evoking mental images helps readers create images in writing.

(Adapted from Keene and PEBC)

Tried and True Texts for Mental Images

Close Your Eyes by Jean Marzollo
Color Me a Rhyme by Jane Yolen
Creatures of Earth, Sea, and Sky by Georgia Heard
Footprints and Shadows by Anne Westcott Dodd
Goodnight to Annie by Eve Merriam
Greyling by Jane Yolen
I Am the Ocean by Suzanna Marshak
Mountain Streams (compact disc)
The Napping House by Audrey Wood
Night in the Country by Cynthia Rylant
Night Sounds, Morning Colors by Rosemary Wells
Putting the World to Sleep by Shelley Moore Thomas
Quiet, Please by Eve Merriam
The Salamander Room by Anne Mazer
Say Something by Mary Stoltz
What Does the Rain Play? by Nancy White Carlstrom
When I'm Sleepy by Jane R. Howard
Wild, Wild Sunflower Child by Nancy White Carlstrom
The Zoo at Night by Martha Robinson

Im PrdCting
Rhoda is not
going to

Cleanup her
room. whi?
Bekos I DONt
Like to clen uP

My room EVr.

C

Children make
predictions based on
personal experience.

Christopher thinking his
way through Judy
Donnelly's *The Titanic
Lost and Found.*

93

Apples, carrots, and yogurt are back in our lunches. Holiday cookies, cakes, and candies are thankfully long gone, along with the mugs that sing while you sip, the very large reindeer pins with blinking noses, and the lovely red sweatshirts with every child's name written in glitter. It's time to get down to business.

"Can you believe it's January already?" we ask each other in the halls. "How can that be," we wonder, "when we have so much left to teach?" We're afraid we'll never get to everything. And we're right—we won't.

In our hearts we know we couldn't even if we tried. We stop to remind ourselves of conversations in faculty meetings, on the stairs, and in the parking lot. We remind ourselves that we believe in depth over breadth; we believe that teaching a few things well makes more sense than teaching many things superficially. And we resolve to continue to do what we believe is best for our kids, our school, and ourselves.

So what's next? By now children know all about thinking about their thinking. They're ready to learn how to engage in deeper, more thoughtful conversations with others and respond to text in ways that increase their capacity for understanding. Now is the time to build on what has come before.

Over the past few months, children have come to know each other well. They know about each other's interests, special talents, and little idiosyncrasies. They know that Adam is the dinosaur expert, Thad is fascinated with JFK, and Paige is a standout soccer player. They've been outraged by the bullies in *Oliver Button Is a Sissy,* sipped hot chocolate together on Coffeehouse Poetry Day, and have had experiences working in a variety of large and small groups. They have history.

And because they do, the time is right for increasing the sophistication of the read-alouds, showing them how to engage in more challenging dialogue and making connections from our past experiences to more in-depth learning.

Taking the Conversation Deeper

It's one thing to share thinking and listen respectfully, and quite another to *listen actively* and *respond thoughtfully* to others in order to understand another's point of view and/or inform one's own. Now is the time to teach children the difference. It's no longer enough for me to ask, "So what are you thinking, Daniel? And Madison? And Frank? And Molly?" Continuing to elicit individual responses without focusing or connecting them does little to extend the conversation, take it deeper, or enhance understanding.

I explain to the children that because they've gotten so good at thinking out loud and listening to each other, they're ready to learn how to listen and learn together in new ways. "You know how readers make connections from the books they read to their lives, other books, and the world?" I ask them. "When readers talk together about books, they make connections from the thinking of others to their own thinking, too. Whether it's to better understand a tricky part of text or talk about a favorite page, thoughtful readers engage in dialogue to better understand books and each other."

The strategies of questioning and inferring are particularly helpful in teaching children how to take the conversation deeper. Asking children to choose a burning question from a chart we've created together, or posing an open-ended question myself and working with them to infer meaning is a perfect way to get started. The question serves to focus the dialogue; showing children how to collaborate to infer answers, solve problems, and construct meaning comes next.

Modeling, naming what I do and what I notice the children doing, and guiding them as needed gets us started. Children aren't raising their hands now. I want them to learn how real conversation flows; I want them to learn how to get it going, keep it going, and take it deeper. I teach children to ask themselves the following questions before joining a conversation:

- Does what I have to say connect to the question or topic?
- Can I connect what I have to say to what someone else has said?
- Can I support what I have to say? What evidence or personal experience do I have to make my point?
- Has someone else already said what I am about to say?
- If I am speaking to disagree, can I state what I heard the other person say and explain how and why my thinking is different in a nice way?
- Does what I want to say take the conversation deeper?

Talking through a text together, working in small groups, getting eye-to-eye and knee-to-knee, and participating in the sharing and the regularly scheduled book clubs allow children to practice and learn the art of collaboration. Whether it's working on an issue on the playground, problem solving in math, hypothesizing in science, or answering a question in reading, children are up to the challenge when we show them how.

I admit it sounds a bit daunting, but year after year I've listened and watched as children work and learn together in ways that exceeded my expectations. So . . . expect brilliance. Model well and model often. Pay attention to detail. Trust yourself and your kids. You won't be disappointed!

Book Clubs for Primary Kids?

It was a speaker at a literacy conference in Denver who inspired me to introduce book clubs to six- and seven-year-olds. She spoke about the rich discussions that were possible for children in the intermediate grades.

"What about primary kids?" I asked her (in my head). "Just because children aren't yet fluent readers doesn't mean they can't think and talk about books in meaningful ways."

I knew then and there that book clubs would soon be coming to my classroom. I'd always wondered how children would talk about books if I weren't there. Would they respond in the same ways they did in the large group? Would they use the same language? Would they talk about their connections, images, questions, and inferences? Maybe book clubs could help me find out.

Over the next few weeks I hatched a plan. I realized that while I still wanted to learn more about how children were applying their learning, more than anything else I wanted to provide a time and place for them to engage in active, lively conversation about books and ideas—without a pre-set agenda. Giving children ongoing opportunities to get together *by themselves* simply to enjoy books and engage in the social nature of learning became my primary goal.

I thought about the book clubs I'd been in over the years. There were the professional ones, where we read only work-related texts. There was the neighborhood one, where we read best-sellers. And there was the one where women's angst reigned supreme.

I thought about my current book club, now in its fifth year. What was it about this one that kept us coming back? I thought it had to do with the diversity of the group and the diversity of the kinds of books we read. The group includes men and women, teachers and stonecutters, journalists, accountants, businesspeople, brokers, and more. Our reading reflects our individual and collective interests. We keep coming back because while we mostly talk about books, we talk about other things, too. We gain new insights, challenge old perspectives, and sometimes feel we've solved the problems of the world. (And then there's the food. . . .)

How can I transport this same kind of spirit into the classroom? I wondered. First, I knew that the kids needed to see and hear what I was talking about. They needed to see a book club like mine in action. To that end, I recruited four parents I knew well—two moms and two dads—and explained what I was after. With only a little arm twisting, they agreed to model a book club with me. I gave them each a copy of *Where the Wild Things Are* along with some sticky notes, and we set a date. It worked so well that I now convene a model book club each year.

On the specified day, we sit in a circle on the floor, with the children sitting in a bigger circle around us. We chat a bit, pass around a snack of animal crackers, and begin talking about the book. (Don't worry—parents never lack for words. One time they went on for thirty minutes just talking about connections! By then the children had themselves become wild things, and I was ready to set sail myself.)

I ask the kids to watch and listen carefully to what the adults do and say. Afterward I write down their observations on chart paper and hang it on the wall near where their own book clubs will meet. The children observe the adults

- working together to figure out answers to questions
- taking turns talking
- asking questions
- laughing
- rereading parts of the book
- making connections from the book to our lives and other books
- inferring
- working together to understand

Children choose their books for the book club from those we've read aloud and discussed previously. That way, they all can discuss books that are sophisticated enough to warrant thoughtful conversation; knowing how to read the book is not a requirement. Multiple copies are kept together in a small bookshelf next to where the book clubs meet.

At first I wondered if having heard and discussed a book before might dampen the children's enthusiasm, but it seems to have just the opposite effect. Their familiarity with the text seems to jump-start the conversation, giving children the confidence they need when the focus of the talk shifts to new issues and ideas.

I meet briefly with each group *the day before* their book club meets and read the text aloud again; children follow along in individual copies. I ask them to bring sticky notes and/or their notebooks with them to the read-aloud so that they can prepare for the next day's discussion by marking the text or otherwise making notes.

Favorite books include the following:

Amazing Grace by Mary Hoffman
An Angel for Solomon Singer by Cynthia Rylant
Grandfather Twilight by Barbara Berger
How Many Days to America? by Eve Bunting
The Lotus Seed by Sherry Garland
The Magic Fish by Freya Littledale
Oliver Button Is a Sissy by Tomie dePaola
Sleeping Ugly by Jane Yolen
The Table Where Rich People Sit by Byrd Baylor
The Titanic Lost and Found by Judy Donnelly
Tut's Mummy Lost and Found by Judy Donnelly
Wild, Wild Wolves by Joyce Milton
William's Doll by Charlotte Zolotow

Over the years I've collected multiple copies of my own, but libraries can help you acquire the copies you need.

Because I want to ensure a mix of boys, girls, interests, and reading abilities, I group children accordingly, four or five per group. One book club meets each week during independent reading time. This gives children a chance to participate every five weeks or so. They meet at a low, round table in the classroom while the rest of us read and confer. Book clubs last anywhere from fifteen to thirty minutes. When the children finish, they reflect aloud on how things went, choose their next book, and rejoin their classmates in readers' workshop.

Are children able to talk together about books and ideas independently and in meaningful ways? Do they talk about their connections, images, questions, and inferences? Yes! And I've come to think I know why. Their knowledge of the language and strategies that readers use propels them into lively conversations as they discuss issues and ideas, gain new insights, and challenge old perspectives. Who knows? One day they might solve the world's problems!

Making Thinking Visible

Once I gave up the basal reader, it took awhile to figure out what kids should be doing instead of those neatly stapled stacks of worksheets. I

Collaborating to compose "Our Promise to Each Other" sets the tone for learning and cooperation early in the year.

What can I do when someone is annoying or hurting me? Look the person in the eye and say nicely,

I don't like it when _____

I feel _____ when you _____

I want _____

When someone tells you this, what can you say back? Look the person in the eye and say nicely,

I heard you say _____

I won't _____

I am sorry.

Giving children a framework for thinking and talking about appropriate ways to ask someone to stop helps build respectful, caring communities.

Our Promise to Each Other

When we care about each other and our classroom, we share what we have, listen carefully, help each other learn, work hard, and have fun together. We understand that everyone makes mistakes, that we stand up for ourselves and others, and when someone asks us to stop, we stop. This is who we are, even when no one is watching!

Promises

Oliver Button Is a Sissy

Creating classroom environments that are literate, organized, purposeful, and accessible nurture literacy and foster independence.

Scissors, markers, glue, crayons, pencils, and sticky notes should always be handy.

Models constructed from clay and paper illustrate a child's learning and demonstrate understanding.

Why are some tornadoes tall and others short?

Bigger winds makes tornadoes taller. Small winds make tornadoes smaller.

Source: Wolrd Book tornadoes 1999.

Children need comfortable, quiet spaces for working in small groups, pairs, and independently.

Reading and thinking aloud gives teachers opportunities to model the cognitive processes used to construct meaning.

Asking children to respond to a read-aloud allows them to focus on the content of the story without being responsible for reading it, too.

Creating environments that nurture literacy and foster independence requires thoughtful planning.

Ben's definition of synthesis.

Knowing ourselves as readers and recording what we've learned about books in the classroom helps readers make good choices.

Hollis and Olivia work to better understand Sherry Garland's *The Lotus Seed* by recording and organizing their questions, mental images, connections, and inferences.

thought that surely they needed to do *something* when they finished reading a book. But what? Design book jackets? Draw a picture of their favorite part? Make puppets of the book's characters? Rewrite endings? My kids did all these things—and loved every minute.

But my colleagues and I began to notice that while it took children ten minutes to read a book, it could take them thirty minutes to design a book jacket. And for what? Most likely it would wind up on a bulletin board underneath a snappy heading. It dawned on me that these activities were keeping children from doing what we know helps them learn to read best: *reading*.

If readers' workshop is all about real reading, it must be about responding in real ways, too. Nowadays when children in my class respond to their reading, the focus is on what they're thinking and learning. Nowadays the purpose of their response is to enhance understanding. And those time-consuming projects? They've gone the way of the worksheets.

Teaching children how to use a variety of open-ended responses helps them remember their thinking as they read, heightens their awareness of the strategy being taught, and lets us (and them) know how well they're able to apply it independently. Ultimately, when that little voice in a child's head says, "What? I don't get this!" responses that focus on thinking and learning can help change that voice to "Oh, I get it now!"

What are the kinds of responses that focus and engage young readers, helping them hold on to their thinking and enhance understanding? Which ones show the children and me how they're applying a strategy and what they're learning and thinking? And which ones are the most universal, able to be used across strategies and throughout the day? Options for response are many, but the following are those I use and teach most consistently:

- Sticky notes. This is probably what kids use most. Keeping track of your thinking on sticky notes is a lot like writing in the margins or highlighting text in your own book. The uses of sticky notes are almost limitless—children use them to record strategy use, draw images, make and confirm predictions, form opinions, think their way through a text, and on and on.
- Notebook entries. I teach children to use their notebooks because of their accessibility and versatility, both at school and at home. Notebooks are great for both written and artistic responses. I some-times ask children to bring their notebooks to a read-aloud to help them keep track of their thinking, record their questions, determine important learning and ideas, synthesize information, and so on.

- Two-column notes. Almost as versatile as sticky notes and notebooks, a two-column setup for notes is also open-ended and can be used in a variety of ways. For example, one column might be headed "Quote from text" and the other, "My thinking"; "I learned"/"I wonder"; "Quote from text"/"My image"; and the like.
- Venn diagrams. These are useful when comparing relationships between pairs of characters, authors, types of text, strategies, and even such specific things as meteors, comets, and asteroids.
- Webs. These are useful in "putting it all out on the table" in the process of answering questions, determining important ideas, drawing inferences, and forming conclusions.
- Story maps. These are useful in helping children understand how story elements work together to create meaning.

I teach children how and when to use each response one at a time. I take my time introducing each one, waiting for just the moment a particular approach will be the most helpful and make the most sense, when the experience might be anchored in the child's mind. That way, when kids encounter similar problems in their own reading, they will connect their current situation to the earlier experience.

Teaching children a new way to respond is not unlike teaching a new strategy. Once I've modeled the response, I need to provide opportunities for children to gradually assume responsibility for its use. In addition to asking them to work through a new response option in small groups and pairs, I sometimes ask them to bring clipboards and pencils to the meeting area, where they'll practice using the response in the course of a read-aloud. This way, their focus can be on listening to the story and using the response rather than having to be responsible for reading the text, too. When children experience and understand the purpose of each response, it becomes easier for them to apply it in their own reading in purposeful ways.

When teaching children how to respond in a new way, I want them to understand that this is now another option, or tool, they can use to help themselves make sense of their reading; it's another technique they can add to those they already know. I want the children to understand how to use each type of response flexibly, to adapt the responses in ways that are most useful, and most important, to create their own ways of building understanding.

For example, after teaching children how to use story maps to identify important information in fiction, I moved into showing them how to identify the key ideas, or themes, in stories. Olivia was puzzled. She brought me

FIGURE 7.1 Olivia's suggestion for the story map form

Story Mapping

Name _Olivia_

Book title _Alot of otters._

The setting	The characters
In the ocin a log time ogow.	A moon, a child and Some otters.

Theme

Keep trak of your babe.

The problem	The solution
The moon child got lost.	The mother fond her in a boxs in the ocbin.

the story map form and said, "Where's the place for the theme? I think it should be on here somewhere." When I asked her where, she didn't hesitate. I incorporated her suggestion on the form that night (Figure 7.1).

Looking closely at children's responses, conferring, listening carefully, and taking notes about what they have to say throughout the day give me a clear indication of where they are as learners, both independently and as a group. I learn which children need more individual or small-group support, and which ones are ready to move forward into more challenging or different types of text.

Taking the Learning Deeper

It's the last forty minutes of the day—work activity time in Room 104. As I take a minute to stand back and reflect, I'm struck by the realization that at this very moment, not one child is calling my name, tugging at my sleeve, or tapping my shoulder. I take the opportunity to pick up my notebook, find a corner, and take a closer look.

I love what I see. Perched on my grandmother's small spindle rocker, Olivia is reading aloud from *Oliver Button Is a Sissy* by Tomie dePaola. Whitney, Jaron, Daniel, and Tate sit cross-legged in a semicircle below her, their fingers following along in copies of the book as she reads. Shoulders straight and legs crossed, Olivia stops reading and puts the book in her lap.

"Now here's what I'm wondering right now," she says in a voice vaguely familiar. "On this page, where the boys took Oliver Button's shoes and wouldn't give them back, I just keep wondering, why would they do that? Why do you think they would do that?"

She's drawn a questioning web on the dry-erase board and written, "Why would they do that?" in the circle at the center. "Maybe they're just jealous of him," Whitney volunteers. "Well, that *could* be it," Olivia responds, as she writes Whitney's response on the web. "What do the rest of you think about that?"

I'd love to know what the rest of them think about that, but Chris catches my eye across the room. Surrounded by a stack of volcano books, he's glued about a mile of red yarn on top of a volcano he's made from brown construction paper, and now he's taping six long pages of writing, end to end, to the volcano's base. Titled "Pompeii Buried Alive!" his piece begins, "A large cloud appeared over the volcano. WOW! I can see the ashes falling on the people and the houses in my head. That had to hurt. . . ."

In another part of the room, Sunny, Paige, Grace, Brodie, Frankie, and Torin are preparing for their play, which was inspired by the book *Heckedy Peg* by Audrey Wood. Copies of the text, along with fabric, thread, needles, paper, staplers, scissors, markers, and glue cover the tabletop as they work to create costumes, props, tickets, scripts, a program, and signs.

The Lego kids are busy, too. Mitchell's building a deinonychus for his dinosaur research ("How can deinonychus run so fast?") and Thad's creating a model of the Texas School Book Depository Building. He's fascinated with JFK and is preparing for a class he'll be teaching this time tomorrow. Five kids and I have signed up already, and he's asked us in writing to bring notebooks, pencils, and "all your questions."

Maggie, Bret, Nina, and Madi are trying to figure out how they can adapt their Irish step dancing moves to the tune "Rockin' Robin," and right behind them Meghan, Nicole, and Caroline are working on their dog research. They've stuffed their notebooks full of dog poems, pictures, notes, and observations, real examples of dog biscuits and treats, and photographs of dogs they know. Today, according to plan, they've brought in samples of hair from all those dogs they know and are sorting them into plastic bags and labeling each bag with a permanent marker.

Whit and Frank are building "Little Bear World" out of wooden blocks, and just outside the room a small chorus of girls and boys are singing their way through their three-ring binders. The binders are filled with copies of the songs we've learned so far, and the children are on the fourth, with about twenty more to go. Cory, Madison, and Kenta gingerly sidestep them on their way out to the playground for gravel and sand. We read *Where Are You Going, Manyoni?* by Catherine Stock earlier and they're intent on creating Tobwani Dam in an old aquarium.

I smile as I watch them, remembering the raised eyebrows of those who earlier in the year wondered how in the world I could find the time to let children "just play"—and every day, too, for goodness' sake.

Work Activity Time

In the beginning of the year, children use work activity time to investigate and explore the materials in the classroom. I explain the options they will have during this part of the day and trust them to make good choices. Together, we work to create the expectations and procedures we will follow. It's a time for building relationships and establishing community, playing together and making new friends, practicing being thoughtful and respectful to each other, and learning the art of sharing a room and everything in it with twenty-six other people.

And it's the perfect time for children to synthesize and apply their learning in new contexts, either independently or with their peers; it's the time when children can put into practice what they've learned during other parts of the day. But before we can expect the Tobwani Dams, Little Bear Worlds, and classes on JFK, children need time to explore, investigate, and yes, play.

They need time to build with blocks, draw, paint, cut and paste, play with clay, make beaded necklaces, finger-knit friendship bracelets, sew, take care of the animals, and listen to stories. They need time to read and write, listen to music, sing and dance, play school, do experiments, work with magnetic letters, and play board games like Sorry, checkers, and chess.

I don't worry about who goes where, for how long, or how many are already there. There are no sign-ups, rotations, or elaborate plans for children to fill out. I simply ask them where they'd like to go and what they'd like to do, and remind them of what we've learned about being respectful and thoughtful to each other and the materials in the classroom.

The principles that guide my work throughout the rest of the day guide my work here, too. Just as in readers' and writers' workshop, providing time, choice, a variety of materials for a wide range of responses, and a predictable structure children can count on allows the unpredictable to happen. If I want to challenge children's imagination, promote their love of learning and inquiry, and encourage them to become independent learners and thinkers, they need to be the ones deciding where they'll go and what they'll do.

And if I'm patient, one fine day someone will think to paint an image from a poem they've written or read, or start a dinosaur book club, or create a cutaway of Earth out of clay. One fine day someone will ask a question about the whereabouts of our missing frog and write a note to everyone to help him infer where it might have gone. And one fine day someone may choose to make a chart that synthesizes her learning about Planet X.

When that day comes, I shout it from the rooftops. I ask the child to share his work, and when he's finished, I say, "How did you come up with such a good idea?" I let everyone know how making connections from what they already know to another situation or time of day is a brilliant thing to do. And because it happens every year, I know that the share circle will soon be filled with other kids who have plenty of brilliant ideas of their own!

Children's talk changes from "I want to make pizzas out of clay" to "I want to make the planets out of clay and put them in order from the sun. And then I want to share it with the kindergartners." Once children begin to integrate their learning into their play, the materials are no longer an end unto themselves; they've become another means for creating understanding and constructing meaning. They've become a means for living the learning.

8

Inferring

Created during work activity time, these posters show how children apply their learning in new settings and situations.

"So what are you inferring this is about?"

105

Cory and Whit rush into the classroom minutes before the bell. They scurry over to a corner, where Cory plunks down his backpack and takes out what looks to be a cell phone. "See, Whit? Here it is. My mom says it's broken, but I'm inferring we can fix it!" Out of the corner of my eye I watch them turn it over and over, furiously pushing buttons, pulling the antennae out and pushing it back in, checking the batteries, listening for a dial tone.

To their surprise (and mine), the phone begins to make a strange beeping sound. "See? I just knew it!" Cory says. "It just needs a little something. Go get a magnifying glass, quick!" They methodically examine every inch (centimeter?) of the phone. But no amount of close examination renders them a dial tone. The beeping stops. "Well, Whit," Cory says softly, "at least we tried."

"Cory," Whit pleads, "we can't give up yet. Oh—wait! I know!" He races over to the basket of two-column note forms and grabs one. "We can infer what's wrong with it!" he says. "Let's put our thinking together. I'll draw the phone on this side, and you write our thinking over here. This is going to be a huge infer! When we figure it out, let's show Mrs. Miller! She'll go crazy for this!" (They were right—see Figure 8.1.)

The children have been learning about the ways readers (and telephone repairmen) infer for about four weeks. When I think about how far the kids

FIGURE 8.1 Cory and Whit's two-column notes on the phone

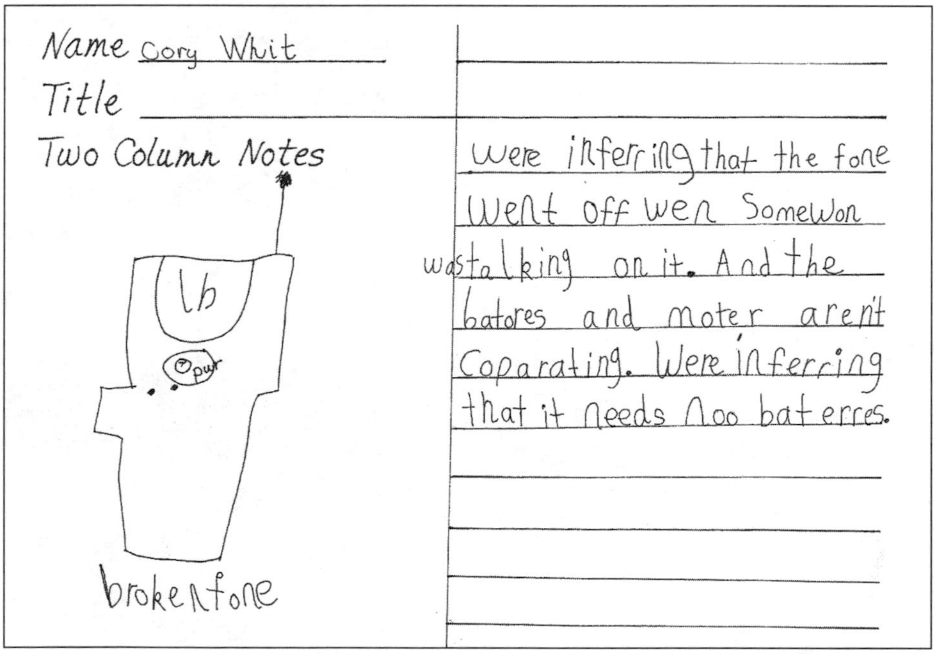
Name Cory Whit
Title
Two Column Notes
Were inferring that the fone Went off wen Somewon was talking on it. And the batores and moter aren't Coparating. Were inferring that it needs noo baterres.
brokenfone

have come, I realize it's because I've come a long way, too. I remember when I wasn't even sure what inferring was, let alone how to go about teaching it.

I think back to the day when ten of us were scrunched into the old book room at University Park Elementary, where PEBC staff developer Chryse Hutchins was leading an after-school discussion on teaching inferring to our first and second graders. "So what's everybody thinking?" she asks us. We love Chryse, but the room is freezing. We think those might be snowflakes outside the window. And we don't really feel like thinking. Chryse knows all about wait time, but so do we. Undeterred, she asks, "So how is inferring going in your classrooms? Who would like to share what you've been doing?" Kristin and I exchange glances. Should we tell?

Kristin gives me a silent kick. I take the cue. I'll tell. "Well, Chryse, I'm confused, actually. Kristin and I have been having this ongoing discussion about inferring, and we've been wondering things like, well, what does it mean to infer? At first we thought it was about predicting, but if a child makes a prediction and confirms it a page later, is that really an inference, or just a simple prediction?" We think inferring is bigger than predicting, but we're not sure.

This conversation took place early in our work with Chryse, and we were surprised to learn that she wasn't sure about the difference either. And she was smart enough to admit it to us. As with the best staff developers, Chryse was one of the first to engage us in conversations in which we all participated in the learning. So what is inferring? Prediction is a piece of it, but our hunches were right: there is more to it. Inferring, according to Anderson and Pearson (1984) is the heart of meaning construction for learners of all ages. What follows are some key considerations and anchor lessons on inferring that put theory into practice. When readers infer, they use their prior knowledge and textual clues to draw conclusions and form unique interpretations of text.

Anchor Lessons

Readers determine meanings of unknown words by using their schema, paying attention to textual and picture clues, rereading, and engaging in conversations with others

A book like *Where Are You Going, Manyoni?* by Catherine Stock is perfect for teaching children about inferring at the word level. Set on the Limpopo River in a dry, sparsely settled area in Zimbabwe, it's the story of a little girl who passes through the veld on her way to school. Along the way, she skips past shady kloofs, red sandstone koppies, acacia and baobab trees, foraging bushpigs, and malala palms, all of which offer opportunities for authentic modeling of how to infer meanings of unknown words.

On the first day, I read aloud the first few pages, thinking aloud about the meanings of words like *baobab, Limpopo,* and *bushpig.* On the page with the baobab tree, I say, "Hmmm. Baobab tree? What kind of tree is that? I think I've heard the word *baobab,* but I'm pretty sure I've never seen a tree by that name. I'm going to reread this page. Let's see, it talks about the *great, grey* baobab tree. I think *great* means *big* in this sentence. When I look at the picture, there's a huge tree that is greyish. See this one? I'm inferring that it is the baobab tree."

After modeling several other words in much the same way, I say, "Think a minute about what you just saw and heard me doing to infer the meanings of words I didn't understand. What did you notice?" Children noticed I was

- rereading
- paying attention to the words
- looking closely at the pictures
- using my schema
- taking my time
- thinking really hard

"Good noticing!" I tell them. "Now it's your turn. Listen carefully as I read, and if you hear a word you don't understand, raise your hand and we'll work together to infer its meaning." I read about halfway through the book, and along the way we infer the meaning of *forages, pan,* and *kloof.* We record our thinking on a chart entitled "What can you do to help yourself figure out the meaning of an unknown word?" The chart is divided into three sections, headed "Word," "What we infer it means," and "What helped us?"

The next day we talk about what we remember and what we learned from our work the day before. I reread the book, and when we get to the part where we left off, I again ask children to raise their hands if they hear a word they don't understand, adding that day's words and our thinking to the chart. At the end of the book we find a glossary of unfamiliar words and their meanings, which gives us an opportunity to confirm or correct some of our definitions on the chart. We decide to mark each with either a **C** when our thinking is confirmed, or a **C** with an **X** on top when our definition is contradicted by the book's glossary.

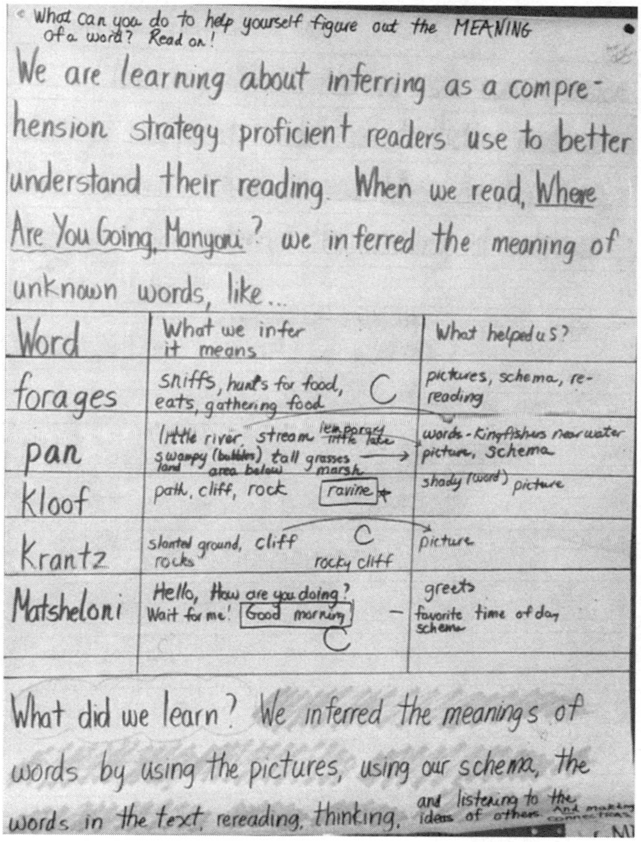

FIGURE 8.2 Inferring meanings of words from *Where Are You Going, Manyoni?* by Catherine Stock

When we finish, I ask the children what they've learned, and I record their thinking on the chart (see Figure 8.2). Before I send them off to readers' workshop I say, "In your reading today, if you come across a word and you don't understand what it means, think about what we've learned and give it a try. Happy reading!"

Postscript: Check out the sticky notes shown in Figure 8.3. A group of kids at one table came up with the sticky note format, and after they shared it with the rest of the class that day, it caught on. Thereafter, children brought their books and sticky notes to share. This allowed us to talk about the meaning of the unknown words together, which gave several children at once a chance to learn new words, and gave me an opportunity to clear up any misconceptions.

Readers make predictions about text and confirm or contradict their predictions as they read on

Books with opportunities for making clear-cut predictions that can be confirmed or contradicted in the text are useful for teaching children about

FIGURE 8.3 Sticky notes to share

prediction. One such book is *The Royal Bee* by Frances and Ginger Park, the story of a young boy in Korea named Song-ho, who wants desperately to learn how to read and write. But only the privileged yangban children are allowed to go to school, and Song-ho is very poor. . . .

I read aloud the first few pages, stopping to infer meanings for such unknown terms as *yangban, sangmin,* and *Royal Bee,* and giving children a bit of background knowledge about the culture of Korea at the time of the story. When we pick up the story again, Song-ho hears the ringing of the school bell off in the distance and follows its sweet sound deep into the valley.

Once there, he looks through the rice-paper doors of the Sodang School and sees the shadows of the yangban pupils and their master. When Master Min slides open the door, Song-ho asks if he can be his pupil. The master admires Song-ho's bravery, but he knows that "rules are rules, and sangmins were not allowed to attend the Sodang School." With a lump in his throat, he tells Song-ho to go home.

I put the book down. "So what are you thinking? What do you predict will happen next?" Grant raises his hand. "I predict Song-ho is going to get into that school, and he's going to learn to read and write poetry."

I record his prediction on a two-column chart entitled "Our predic-tions—and the thinking behind them" and ask, "What's the thinking behind your prediction, Grant? What made you predict that Song-ho will get to go to the Sodang School, even though Master Min tells him to go home?"

"Well, you know how the star of the book always gets the really good stuff? That's why I think he'll get to go."

"That's smart, Grant. You're using your schema for stories like this one to predict what might happen.

"Does anybody have a *different* prediction?" I ask, hoping to see at least one raised hand. But it's not to be. This day everyone predicts that Song-ho is going to the Sodang School, and he's going to learn to read and write!

"Let's go back into the text," I say. "Listen as I reread and see if you hear anything else that might have helped you predict he'd get to go to school and learn to read and write." I add the children's thinking and mine to the chart, right under Grant's. As we read on, the children confirm their prediction when Master Min says, "Welcome to the Sodang School, Song-ho." I put a **C** for "confirmed" under their prediction.

The second day I read the rest of the story. Just as we predicted, Song-ho learns to read and write. We learn about the Royal Bee, a contest of knowledge held every spring in the Great Hall at the governor's palace. Only one pupil will be chosen to represent the Sodang School.

I close the book and give children the two-column note form, asking them to predict who will go to the Royal Bee on one side and to record the thinking behind their prediction on the other. (An example of their responses is shown in Figure 8.4.) We share, and then I read the rest of the story aloud. Guess who gets a big cheer when I finish the story? Could it be Song-ho?

Readers use their prior knowledge and textual clues to draw conclusions and form unique interpretations of text

Once I saw the glee on the faces of those "fish" flailing around the meeting area (see Chapter 6), I knew I needed to provide children regular opportu-nities for dramatic expression. But it was Frank's question about the pagoda that kept me thinking. With practice, could dramatic responses really help kids draw conclusions and form unique interpretations of text? Could act-ing out a tricky word or a puzzling piece of text really serve as a means to understanding? Could one child's images build or strengthen the images of another, thereby enhancing their learning?

FIGURE 8.4 Zach's prediction about Song-ho

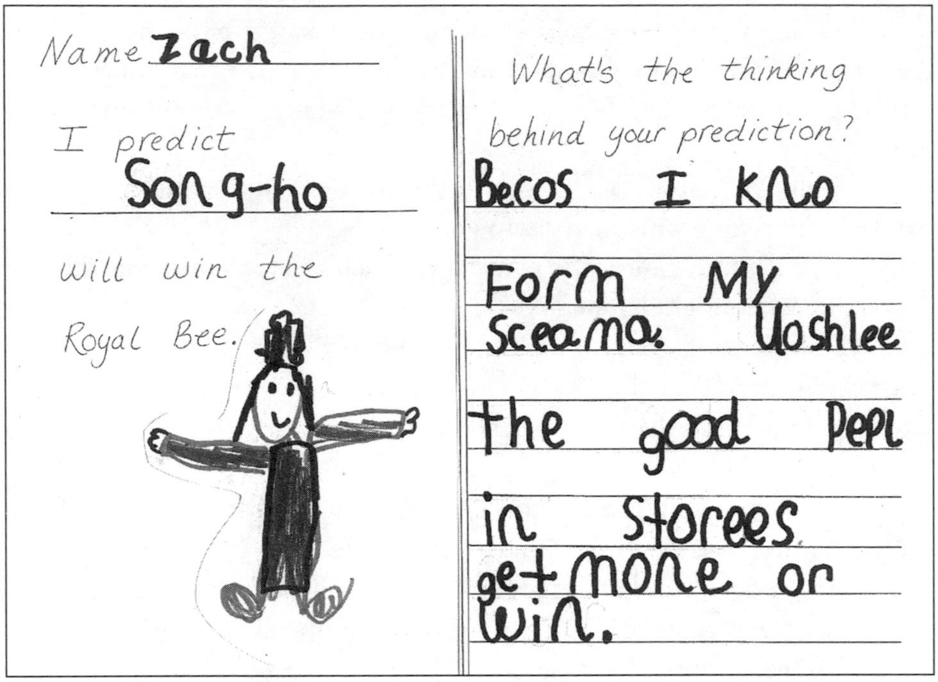

Name **Zach**

I predict
Song-ho

will win the
Royal Bee.

What's the thinking
behind your prediction?
Becos I kno

Form My
sceama. Uoshlee

the good Pepl

in storees
get more or
win.

Frank and the pagoda experience showed me that these activities could help kids—but I had to figure out how I could involve everyone in a manageable way. Again I took up Georgia Heard's book of poems, *Creatures of the Earth, Sea, and Sky.* The poems are short, I know children have at least some schema for most entries, and the content is just difficult enough for children to have to think through the poem carefully to understand it.

I choose six poems I think lend themselves best to dramatic interpretation and copy them onto chart paper. The children and I read each of them aloud several times. Then I say, "Think carefully about the poems we just read. Which one of them is most interesting to you? Which one makes you think, 'Hmmm, what is this poem really about?' Choose one you'd like to understand better.

"Once you've decided, go to the poem you want to learn more about. Take it with you and find a place in the room you can work well. You have about fifteen minutes to build on each other's ideas and figure out how your group can best interpret the poem you've chosen. Good luck!"

I observe Mitchell, Geoffrey, and Allan. They've chosen the poem "Dressing Like a Snake":

A snake changes its clothes
only twice a year.
Beginning with its nose,
peeling down to its toes:
new clothes suddenly appear.
Wouldn't it be nice
to dress only twice
instead of each day of the year?

"What will they do with this one?" I wonder. "Do they get the fact that it's about a snake shedding its skin? What conclusions will they draw? And how in the world will they create an interpretation that mirrors those conclusions?"

I tell myself to stay out of it, and once again, it's a wise decision. Figure 8.5 shows the three boys acting out the snake's shedding its skin.

Children love to use a two-column format to help them organize their thinking as they practice inferring (see Figure 8.6). They mark up the text, record their thinking as it evolves, and in the end come up with what they think the poem or text is about.

Postscript: Children saw these exercises as riddles, and spontaneously began writing their own during writers' workshop. We decided to write a poem together and send it home to see if their parents could figure out what we were describing. This was such a hit that I began to post the

FIGURE 8.5 Mitchell, Geoffrey, and Allan "Dressing Like a Snake"

FIGURE 8.6 Using a two-column format for inferring

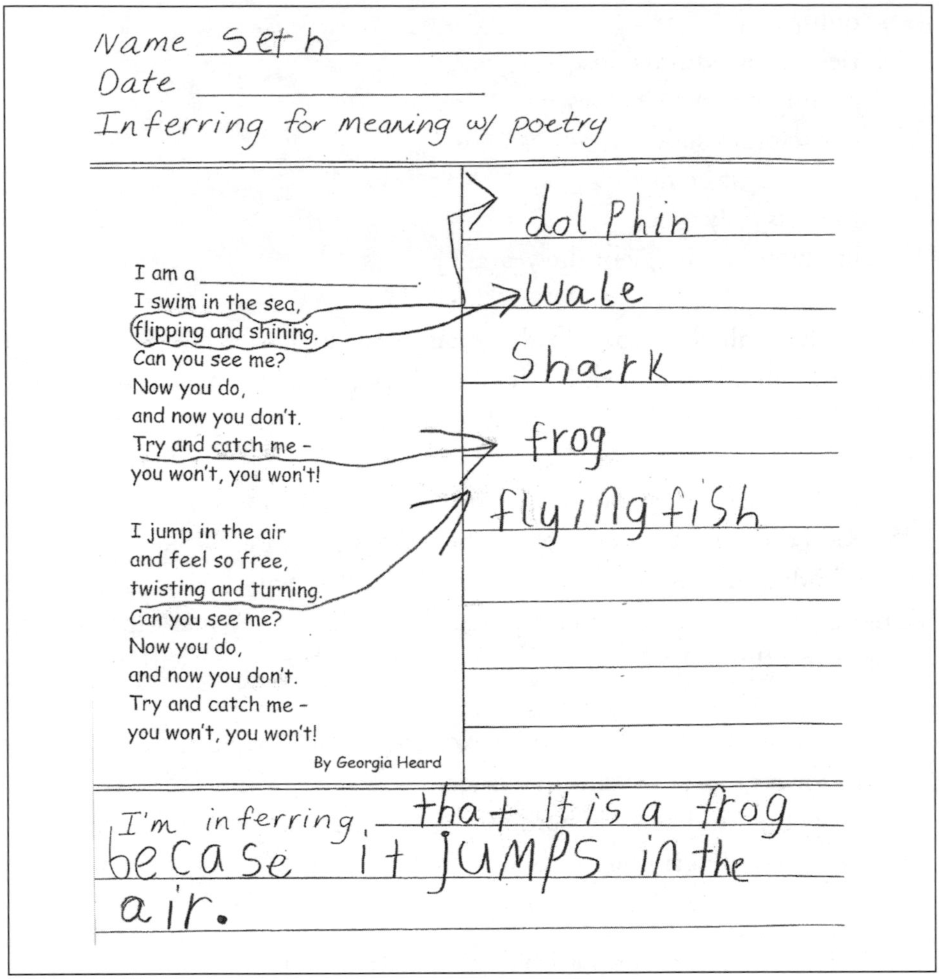

Name _Seth_

Date _____

Inferring for meaning w/ poetry

I am a _____.
I swim in the sea,
~~flipping and shining.~~
Can you see me?
Now you do,
and now you don't.
Try and catch me –
you won't, you won't!

I jump in the air
and feel so free,
twisting and turning.
Can you see me?
Now you do,
and now you don't.
Try and catch me –
you won't, you won't!

By Georgia Heard

dolPhin

wale

Shark

frog

flyingfish

I'm inferring, that it is a frog becase it JUMPS in the air.

children's riddles out in the hall, with spaces for passersby to write in what they inferred the poems were about. After a week or so, children wrote in the titles of their poems, giving those same passersby a chance to confirm or change their thinking.

Readers know to infer when the answers to their questions are not explicitly stated in the text

How Many Days to America? by Eve Bunting is the story of a family forced by soldiers to flee the village they love. They board a small fishing boat in the middle of the night, taking with them only a change of clothing and some jewelry to buy their way to America. The trip is a dangerous one; the motors of the little boat stop, the passengers run out of food and water, and thieves come aboard, demanding money and jewels. Will they ever reach America safely?

I choose a book like this one because I know the story will provoke lots of questions, most of them requiring readers to infer answers by using clues in the text and their prior knowledge. I know, too, that because the content is difficult, there will be opportunities for teaching children to actively listen and learn from each other.

I begin by reading aloud and modeling my questions. Three or four pages in, I invite children to share their questions; I add them to mine in my notebook. By the end of the story, we've asked many questions:

- Why did the soldiers make them leave?
- Why did she have to give him her wedding ring? And garnets?
- Why are the soldiers shooting at them instead of helping?
- Did they go to our America? We don't have trees like that.
- Where are they from?
- Why did the thieves steal from them? They were so nice.
- Will they ever get to America?
- Did they get to go back to their village?

After school I write the questions on a chart, and we take a couple of days to go back into the text to work together to figure out the answers. I think aloud about how I'm using my schema, the pictures, and the words in the text to help me infer answers; gradually I invite children to do the same, recording our thinking on the chart. Focusing on one question at a time allows me to show children how to extend dialogue by building on the conversation of others.

Readers create interpretations to enrich and deepen their experience in a text

Have you ever read a book that changed the way you thought or felt about something? Have you ever read a book that made you feel you were a better person for having read it? Maybe you learned something about yourself that you never knew before, looked at an issue from another point of view, or changed your thinking about something you once believed to be true.

Growing up in the small town of Lamar, Colorado, I would sometimes explore with my family the crumbling ruins of nearby Camp Amache, a Japanese internment camp set in the sand and sage of southeastern Colorado. Sitting under the lone cottonwood tree, I'd listen to stories of how this land once held hundreds of Japanese Americans against their will during World War II. I learned that the fear they might in some way contribute to the Japanese war effort was the sole reason for their confinement.

"This happened in America?" I wondered. I couldn't believe it. But when I read James Bradley's *Flags of Our Fathers,* I gained a new perspective. Though the story was still hard to believe, I was at least able to understand the motivation and fears of those who believed that confinement of these U.S. citizens was necessary.

Books like *Miss Maggie* by Cynthia Rylant, *Something Beautiful* by Sharon Dennis Wyeth, *If You Listen* by Charlotte Zolotow, *Oliver Button Is a Sissy* by Tomie dePaola, and *Fireflies* by Julie Brinkloe, whose characters experience the ups and downs of childhood, might help children gain new perspectives. *Miss Maggie* is a story about Maggie Ziegler, an elderly eccentric who lives by herself in a rotting old house out in the middle of nowhere, and Nat Crawford, a little boy who learns to follow his heart when Miss Maggie needs him most.

Before I begin reading, I talk to children about how authors often want their readers to take something away from their book, that they want to leave their readers with something to think about and remember. "Books," I tell them, "can help you think about important things in new ways. As I read *Miss Maggie,* be thinking about what Cynthia Rylant might want you to think about and remember." Devon's written response to this book is shown in Figure 8.7.

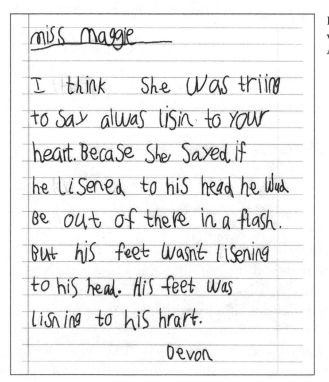

FIGURE 8.7 Devon's written response to *Miss Maggie* by Cynthia Rylant

Evidence of Understanding and Independence

Inferring about a missing frog

When I read thes words Nobody wears a sunsuit on the First day of school. I said claude i prdicktid Claude wod say anthr mean word To Timothy.

Zachary's prediction in *Timothy Goes to School* by Rosemary Wells

"Inferring is thinking in your head to help you understand, when the story doesn't let you in on it."
Colin

"When we infer together, it's like a wire that connects from my head to someone else's head, on and on and on, all around the circle."
Riley

"Inferring is something I always keep with me—wherever I go, it follows me around. I carry it with me to figure out things in my life."
Frank

"You know when you wonder why? If the book doesn't tell you, you can use your schema and the clues in the text to help you. That's inferring."
Nina

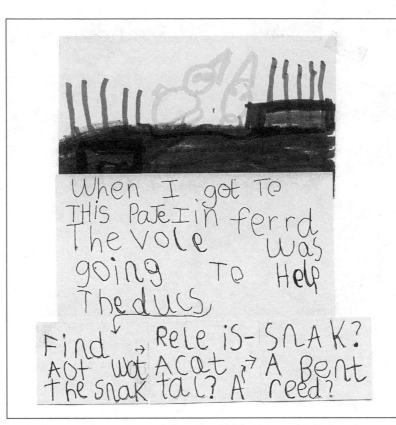

Zach's thinking after reading *Dibble and Dabble* by Dave and Julie Saunders

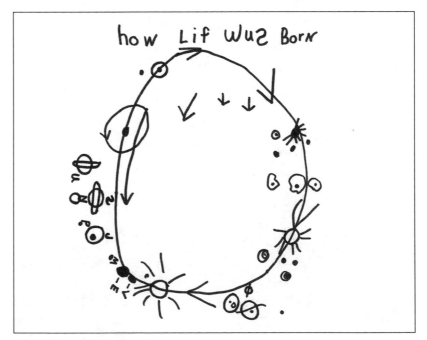

Max's "How Life Was Born"

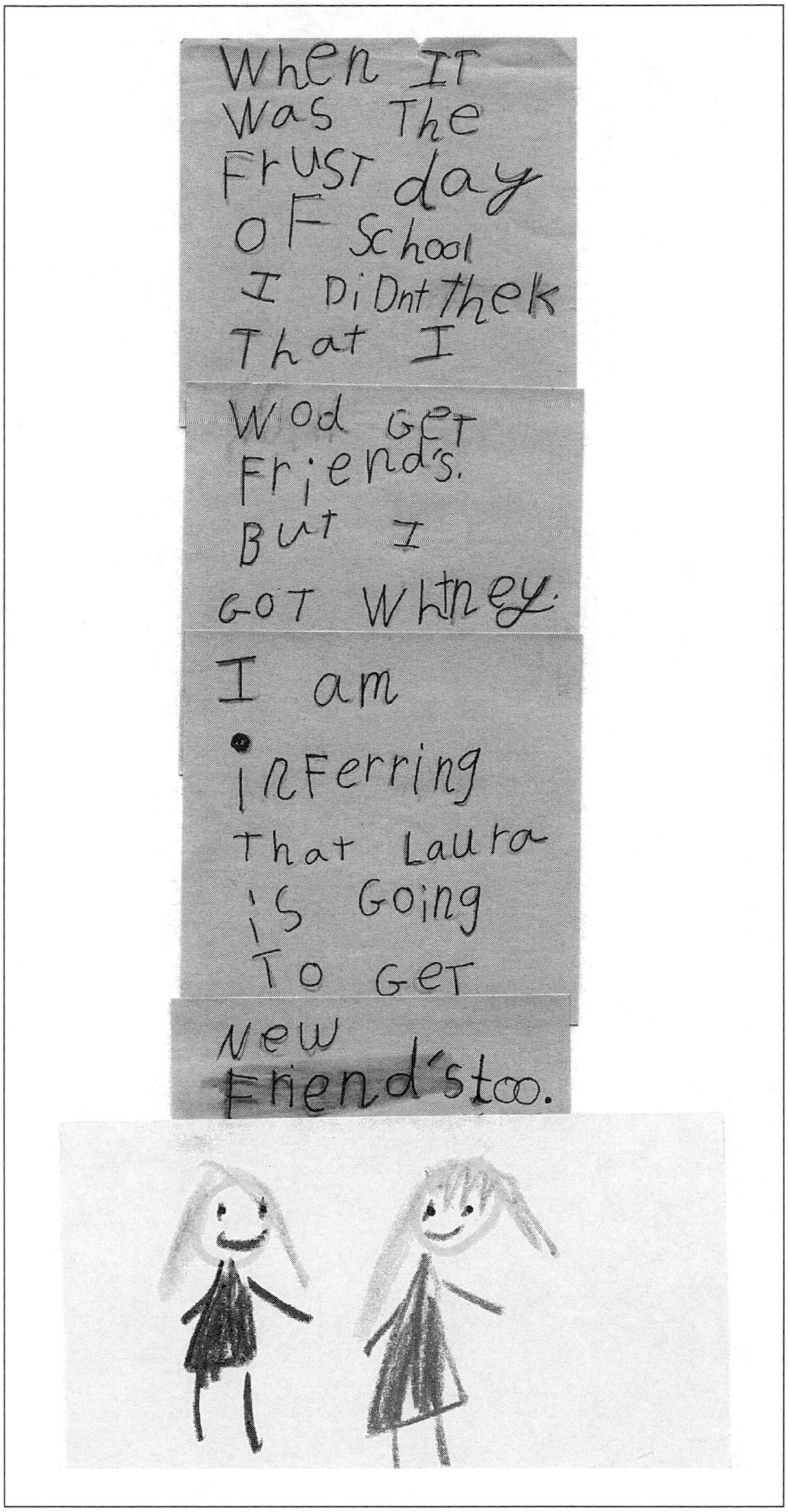

When IT
was The
FrUST day
OF school
I DiDnt thek
That I

wod get
Friends.
BUT I
GOT whitney.

I am
inFerring
That Laura
is Going
To GeT
New
Friend'stoo.

Nina makes connections from her life to the text to enhance understanding

We were inferring
that the frog was
going to feel rane
Drop's But they
were not ran Drop's.

they were teers
from Peache With
her eys shut totilley.

Abby and Emily's inference in *Peach and Blue* by Sarah Kilborne

Inferring at a Glance

What's Key for Kids?

- Readers determine meanings of unknown words by using their schema, paying attention to textual and picture clues, rereading, and engaging in conversations with others.
- Readers make predictions about text and confirm or contradict their predictions as they read on.
- Readers use their prior knowledge and textual clues to draw conclusions and form unique interpretations of text.
- Readers know to infer when the answers to their questions are not explicitly stated in the text.
- Readers create interpretations to enrich and deepen their experience in a text.

(Adapted from Keene and PEBC)

Tried and True Texts for Inferring

Creatures of Earth, Sea, and Sky by Georgia Heard
Fireflies by Julie Brinkloe
Fly Away Home by Eve Bunting
For the Good of the Earth and Sun by Georgia Heard
Grandfather Twilight by Barbara Berger
How Many Days to America? by Eve Bunting
If You Listen by Charlotte Zolotow
Miss Maggie by Cynthia Rylant
Mother Earth, Father Sky selected by Jane Yolen
Oliver Button Is a Sissy by Tomie dePaola
The Royal Bee by Frances Park and Ginger Park
Something Beautiful by Sharon Dennis Wyeth
Where Are You Going, Manyoni? by Catherine Stock
Winter Fox by Catherine Stock

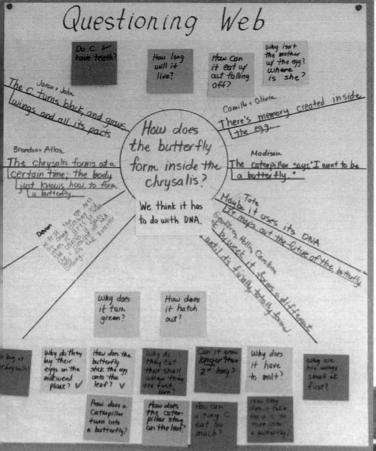

Questioning Web

How does the butterfly form inside the chrysalis?

We think it has to do with DNA.

Jaron + John
The C. turns black and grows wings and all its parts

Brandon + Allan
The chrysalis forms at a certain time; the body just knows how to form a butterfly.

Camille + Olivia
There's memory created inside the egg

Madison
The caterpillar says "I want to be a butterfly."

Tate
Maybe it uses its DNA
If it maps out the future of the butterfly

Do C. have teeth?

How long will it live?

How can it eat w/ out falling off?

Why isn't the mother w/ the egg? Where is she?

Why does it turn green?

How does it hatch out?

Why do they lay their eggs on the milkweed plant? ✓

How does the butterfly stick the egg onto the leaf? ✓

Why do they eat their shell when they are first born?

Can it grow longer than 2" long?

Why does it have to molt?

Why are his wings small at first?

How does a caterpillar turn into a butterfly?

How does the caterpillar stay on the leaf?

How can a tiny C. eat so much?

9

Asking Questions

Questioning webs help children activate and organize their thinking and learning in order to answer a specific question.

Ben and his Wonder Box.

Yikes! This is one weird book," I think as I read *The Stranger* by Chris Van Allsburg late one night. "What's it about?" I wonder, and "What's the deal with the guy?"

"How many times are you going to read that?" my husband asks, sleepily rolling over and pulling a pillow over his head. "Come on," I say. "I know it's late, but just listen to a little of it—there's this one part I want to talk with you about." I take his silence to mean "I'd love to listen and share my thinking with you," so I begin reading aloud. When I finish, I realize he hasn't heard a word.

"Mesmerized" would be how I'd describe the children as they listened to the story the next day. (At least *they* know a good story when they hear one.) And the questions! "Who is the stranger?" many wondered as they sat eye-to-eye and knee-to-knee. "Do you think he's part of nature? Is he magic? Why would Farmer Bailey let a stranger into his house? How could the thermometer break like that?" Their questions seemed endless.

In the midst of the hubbub, Grace plopped herself into my lap and asked, "Mrs. Miller, what are you wondering?"

"Well, you know the part where the stranger is dressed in his old clothes and he's getting ready to leave? I'm wondering what made him decide to go."

"I know why!" she says, opening the book to the page where the stranger is holding the red leaf. "He had to go because he got his memory back. See the red leaf? Remember how it was green? When he blew on it and it turned red, he got his memory back. See his face? The red leaf made him remember who he was."

"How had I missed that?" I wondered. "And how had Grace figured it out so quickly?" I'd always told children that our class is a community of learners and that I had so much to learn from them, but did I really believe it? I was good at listening to children in order to inform my teaching, but did I ever really consider that a child, and an emergent reader at that, could help me understand a picture book?

I don't think so. Grace taught me I don't have to know all the answers to teach well. Understanding that I can be both teacher *and* learner has broadened my definition of my role in the classroom and increased my capacity to teach and learn.

It used to be that the books I deemed weird, or the ones that kept me a little off balance, remained on the shelves of libraries and bookstores. But now they're on my shelves, too. They've become the vehicle that propels my teaching (and learning) forward.

I learned that as my questions became less literal and more sophisticated, so did the children's; as I began to think more deeply about my reading and learning, so did they; and as I began to ask questions that truly mattered to me, they did, too.

Coincidence? Not a chance. The connection is absolute. The children I teach are limited only when I choose to limit myself. And that hardback copy of *The Stranger* propped up on the ledge behind my desk? Call it a reminder.

Anchor Lessons

Readers purposefully and spontaneously ask questions before, during, and after reading

Grandfather Twilight is one of my favorite books for teaching children about asking questions. Beautifully written and illustrated by Barbara Berger, it's the story of Grandfather Twilight and how he puts the world to sleep night after night.

Before reading the book, I explain to the children that thoughtful readers ask questions not only as they read, but also before and after reading. "Like right now," I say, "I'm thinking some of you might have a question or two in your head about this book, *Grandfather Twilight*. Is that true? You *all* do? I really love what great thinkers you are. . . ."

I record our questions, and the children help me code them as we go, putting a **B** for questions we asked *before* we read, a **D** for those we asked *during* reading, and an **A** for those we asked *after* reading the book.

At the end of the read-aloud, our chart looks like this:

We are learning that readers ask questions before, during, and after reading. As we read *Grandfather Twilight,* we wondered:

B What is twilight?
B Is that Grandfather Twilight on the cover?
B I wonder if he's magic.
D What does *among* mean?
D Is this about God?
D How could the strands of pearls be endless?
D How does the pearl get bigger and bigger?
A Why would this author write a book about stuff she doesn't understand?
A Could this be true?

Children notice right away that we'd asked questions before, during, and after reading, but I'm after more. "Here's something else I want you to think about," I say. "*Why* do you think readers ask questions before, during, and after reading? How does asking questions help you become a better reader?" Then I wait. And wait. And wait.

Finally, Madison raises her hand. "I'm thinking it keeps your head in the book. You don't want to stop reading because when you ask questions, you want to find out about them and you just can't stop. It keeps your mind awake."

Postscript: To keep track of the children's thinking and learning throughout this study, I begin a chart entitled "Thinking about Questioning." I divide the chart into thirds, with these headings:

- What do we know about asking questions?
- How does asking questions help the reader?
- How do readers figure out the answers to their questions?

We add to our knowledge during subsequent lessons when I ask, "What did we learn about asking questions today? What new learning could we add to our chart?" Asking children questions like these gives them opportunities to process their learning and gives me a chance to mention what I notice, too. We record our new learning on sticky notes and place them under the appropriate category (see Figure 9.1).

Readers ask questions for many reasons
Readers ask questions to

- clarify meaning.
- speculate about text yet to be read.
- determine an author's style, intent, content, or format.
- focus attention on specific components of the text.
- locate a specific answer in the text or consider rhetorical questions inspired in the text.

Because it's difficult to predict the kinds of questions children might ask, and it seems at odds with good teaching to limit their questions to a certain kind or category, I don't go down this list and focus on the reasons readers ask questions one by one. But I do want children to understand that readers ask different kinds of questions for a variety of purposes. How do I go about it?

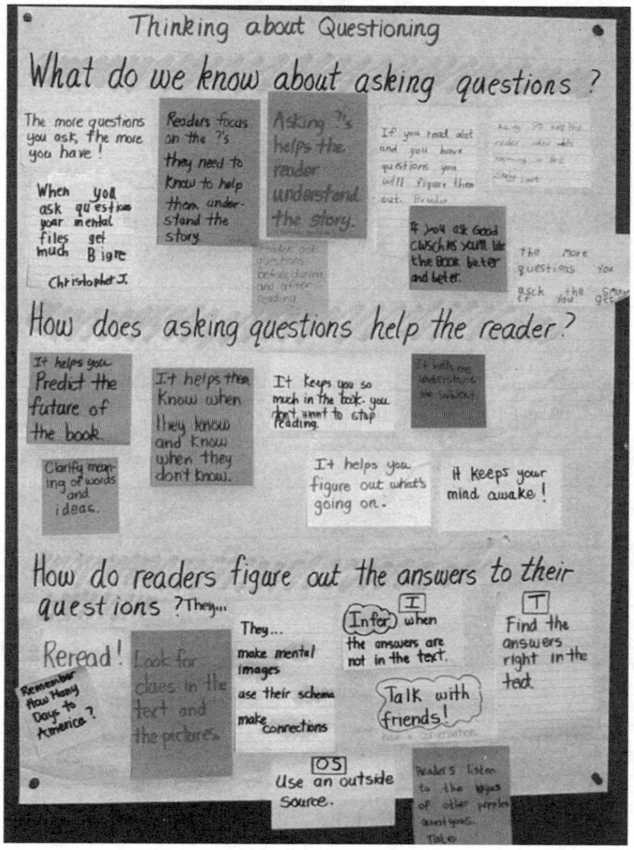

FIGURE 9.1 The "Thinking about Questioning" chart

Throughout our study of questioning, I pay attention to the kinds of questions the children and I ask, pointing out their specific purposes in the moment. We make note of them and add our findings to the chart, right under "How does asking questions help the reader?"

For example, when Meghan says, "I wonder if this book by Jonathan London is going to be like the other Froggy books," I point out that Meghan is asking a question to determine the story's content; she's wondering if her book will be like the others she's read by this author. Or when Maddy asks, "What does 'it is the flower of hope' mean?" I point out that smart readers also ask questions when the meaning of the text is unclear.

Readers determine whether the answers to their questions can be found in the text or whether they will need to infer the answer from the text, their background knowledge, and/or an outside source

The Lotus Seed by Sherry Garland is the story of a Vietnamese family forced to flee their homeland when a devastating civil war breaks out in their country. With soldiers clamoring at their door, they're allowed only a few possessions before scrambling onto a crowded boat and setting sail in stormy seas for America.

Sound familiar? I knew the children, too, would make connections from Eve Bunting's *How Many Days to America?* to *The Lotus Seed.* And I knew they'd have many questions about the content of the story, which would give me a chance to demonstrate that while some answers would require us to infer or consult an outside source, others could be found right in the text.

I record the children's questions before, during, and after reading. Over the next several days we work through them, rereading the text (it's short) and thinking aloud about how we answered many of them. Coding answers with a **T** for those found in the text, an **I** for those we needed to infer, and an **OS** for those requiring an outside source helps make the process visible and increases children's awareness of how and why readers use a variety of strategies to find answers to their questions.

I'm in no hurry for us to get through the questions, nor is recording the answers my primary goal. I want to show kids that thoughtful readers, readers like themselves, not only take the time to ask questions, but also are compelled to seek the answers, even (especially?) when it takes a bit of doing.

At the end of the third day, our chart looks like this:

We are learning that readers figure out the answers to their questions by rereading and looking for clues in the text (**T**), inferring (**I**), and/or using an outside source (**OS**). When we read *The Lotus Seed,* we asked these questions and coded how we figured out their answers.

Where does this take place? **T**
What's a lotus seed? **OS** (Hollis brought one in!)
What is a dragon throne? **T** (author's note)
Who stole it? How did he lose it? **T** (author's note)
What's an altar? **T** (picture in text)
Why did her parents choose her husband for her? **OS** (Mrs. Miller's schema)
Why did he march off to war? Did he die? **I**
Why did she take the lotus seed, but not her mother-of-pearl hair comb? **I**
What does *scrambled* mean? **OS** (Brendan)

What will happen to them? **T**
Who's throwing the bombs? What war is this? **T/OS** (author's note
    and Mrs. Miller)
Where are they going? **T**
What city is this? **I**
Why did they all live together? **I**
Who is Ba'? Why did she cry and cry? **I**
What does "it is the flower of hope" mean? **I**
Why doesn't the author give us more information? **I**
Where is Vietnam? **OS** (globe, pull-down map)

Postscript: One would think that after three days of delving into a
book, children would be ready to move on. Most are, but there are
always some who can't seem to get enough of one book or another. Four
days later, Hollis, Tate, Olivia, and Emily were still poring over *The Lotus
Seed.*

They fashioned a response sheet by connecting five pieces of 12-by-
18-inch construction paper lengthwise with tape; then they covered it
with sticky notes that recorded their thinking. Entitled "Our Thinking
about *The Lotus Seed,*" the sheet bears evidence that these four are using
strategies flexibly—they are on their way to learning how readers purposefully use a variety of strategies *when they need them* to construct
meaning.

They had asked questions, such as

Why did her parents get to choose her husband? We still don't get
    that.
Why didn't the little boy just ask to see the lotus seed?
Why did he hide it?
When Mrs. Miller was reading us *The Lotus Seed,* we didn't know
    what the River of Perfumes meant, and we still don't.
Who is the new emperor?
Where did they go in America?
How many kids did she have?

They had created mental images, drawing pictures of

the lotus flower
red bombs exploding everywhere
an ao dai

grandmother shouting (her mouth one big circle) when she couldn't
    find the lotus seed
an altar

They had drawn inferences, such as

We are inferring she ended up in New York because of all the tall
    buildings and the twinkling blinking lights.
We're thinking she has two or four other kids because in the picture
    there might be some in front of her and some in the back of her
    holding onto her hands.

They had made connections, such as

When I feel lonely or sad, I cuddle up with my blanket or pillow, and
    then I feel safe.
These soldiers are just like the ones in *How Many Days to America?*

They gave opinions, such as

We don't ever want our parents to pick our husbands!
We think *The Lotus Seed* is the best book we've ever read!

Readers understand that many of the most intriguing questions are not answered explicitly in the text, but are left to the reader's interpretation

All I See by Cynthia Rylant is the story of a man named Gregory, who spends his days painting whales. He paints them by the side of a beautiful lake, sometimes whistling a theme from Beethoven's Fifth Symphony, his cat curled up at his feet. When he tires, he lies flat in his canoe and drifts down the lake, smiling up at the sky. A little boy named Charlie watches him from a distance, and the two become great friends.

Experience tells me that the answers to children's questions about stories like this one are not likely to be found in the text. Nor will they be easy to infer. We'll never know for sure why whales are all Gregory sees, if this is his "real job," or what Charlie's passion will be. But thoughtful readers don't just shake their heads in confusion and keep on reading. Thoughtful readers know how intriguing it is to take the time to speculate about these kinds of questions and create their own unique explanations, or interpretations.

"Remember when we created dramatic interpretations of poems?" I ask. "Interpreting answers to questions that are hard to figure out is a lot like that. Readers create their own unique interpretations by using their schema, creating mental images, and talking with others to figure out what makes the most sense to them.

"Let's choose a question from our list," I continue, "one that we really want to figure out, and think out loud about how we might make sense of it."

I've made a questioning web—a circle with lines fanning out from all sides—and I write the question the children choose ("Why are whales all he sees?") inside the circle. I record their interpretations on the lines around it. They think that maybe . . .

- He doesn't want to forget about whales, and he doesn't want the rest of the world to either.
- He has so much schema about whales, he just has to let some of it out.
- He's like a machine full of mental images, and they are all of whales.
- He's passionate about whales.
- The music is an invisible net for mental images—it traps them and helps him see whales.
- If you care about something a lot, you see it everywhere!
- He knows the blue whale is endangered—maybe he wants other people to know it, too, so somebody can do something.
- He's an illustrator for books about whales. Maybe he's friends with Seymour Simon.

When we finish, we talk about all the different ways we've come to think about, or interpret, the question. Sometimes we consider all our different ways of thinking to create a class interpretation; other times we focus on a single one.

Questioning webs are also useful with poetry and nonfiction text (our web in response to *Monarch Butterfly* by Gail Gibbons is shown at the start of this chapter). Children use questioning webs independently, too. For example, Matthew's response to his question "Why is Amelia Bedelia so weird?" is shown in Figure 9.2.

Readers understand that hearing others' questions inspires new ones of their own; likewise, listening to others' answers can also inspire new thinking

What do you do when you have questions in your reading that you just can't figure out? I usually talk with somebody who's read the book (though

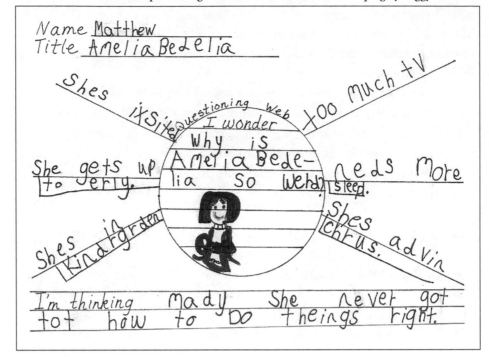

that usually results in even more questions!), or I try to force my best friend to listen to me read aloud at 11:30 P.M. (with limited results).

In the classroom, inviting children to choose a question that is particularly puzzling and get together with a few others who are likewise intrigued provides opportunities for children to think and learn together. This type of activity promotes the social nature of learning in authentic ways and permits children to gain control of a strategy with the support of their peers.

As I listen in on the conversations, sometimes their thinking seems off the mark, and sometimes I think they're right on. But what I believe to be true isn't important at that point; it's the process of children working together to actively construct meaning *for themselves* that is key. Reminding myself that there usually isn't just one right answer keeps me from trying to influence the children's thinking. My advice? Resist the temptation to jump in and lead the kids to what you believe—you may be surprised at what you learn!

I've chosen Cynthia Rylant's *An Angel for Solomon Singer,* the story of a lonely man who lives in a hotel for men in New York City. Solomon Singer wanders the city streets, longing for his boyhood home in Indiana and dreaming of the things he loves: fireplaces, purple walls, porch swings, and balconies. One night he happens into the Westway Café, a place known for making dreams come true. A friendly waiter named Angel tells him to come back, and night after night he does. Soon Solomon Singer's life begins to change. . . .

Children wonder:

- Will there really be an angel in this story?
- Why doesn't Solomon Singer move back with his parents in Indiana?
- How could Indiana be mixed into his blood?
- Why doesn't he come to Colorado? We have hotels here with balconies and purple walls.
- Why does he keep coming back to the Westway Café?
- Is the waiter really an angel?
- Did his dreams come true?

We talk about the questions a bit, and I ask the children to think about which ones seem the most intriguing: "Which one would you most like to talk about with someone else?" I record their choices.

"Listen again to the story," I say to them the next day, "and when I finish, get together with the children who are interested in discussing the same question as you are. I've written the questions and the names of the children who have chosen them on construction paper envelopes like this one. The paper inside is for you to record your thinking *and* anything new you wonder about. Be ready to share your work in about twenty minutes."

Sometimes I ask the children to record their answers first, share them with their group, then record their thinking again, noting how or whether their answers have changed, and why. I also encourage children who are reading the same book independently to get together in small groups to share their questions and ideas.

■ ■ ■

I design lessons like the one that follows to provide one last scaffold before I ask children to apply a strategy independently. The lesson also helps me assess which children may need extra support in small-group work and/or individual conferences.

I choose *Amelia's Road* by Linda Altman because I know that while children will identify with Amelia, her parents, and her teacher, they'll also have questions about migrant farmworkers, labor camps, and why a little girl cries every time her father takes out a road map.

I've prepared a chart and a record sheet for children that are almost identical. Over the span of two or three days, everything we do together in the large group I ask children to do in their own reading as well. For example, on the first day, we

- read the story aloud.
- record our questions on sticky notes.
- place them on the chart.
- choose a burning question we want to focus on the next day.

After the lesson, children do the same things—they

- read independently.
- record their questions on sticky notes.
- place them on their record sheets.
- choose a burning question each wants to focus on the next day.

The next day we reread the story, focusing on our burning question. We work together to answer the question and spend time reflecting on what helped us most. The children then respond in writing to their individual questions during independent reading time and reflect on what helped them most. (See the class chart of *Amelia's Road* and Cory's corresponding response to *Tut's Mummy Lost and Found* at the start of Chapter 1.)

Readers understand that the process of questioning is used in other areas of their lives, both personal and academic

Ben is balanced in the crook of a tree (as shown at the beginning of this chapter). Emily has a magnifying glass and is looking closely at a ladybug. Val's examining a leaf with curious lumpy growths, and Nina's on her back, hands behind her head, looking up at the sky. Ben, Madi, Val, Nina, and their twenty-three classmates are scattered across the school's front lawn, wandering, wondering, and exploring the world around them.

Each has a Wonder Box—a 3-by-5-inch file box they've decorated with small stick-on ladybugs, dinosaurs, birds, and flowers and filled with a stack of brightly colored index cards—"Wonder Cards"—on which to record their questions.

I've just read *The Wise Woman and Her Secret* by Eve Merriam, the story of a wise woman who knows the secret of wisdom and a little girl named Jenny, who learns that she knows the secret, too.

As the children wander, they record questions on their Wonder Cards:

- How does a bird learn to sing?
- Why do ladybugs have spots?
- Are we right now out in space?
- How does an ant find its way home?
- How was the world born?
- Why do trees have bark?
- Why do dogs have wet noses?
- Why do some leaves have lumps?
- Who made God?
- Why is the sky blue?
- Why do bees sting?
- Did dinosaurs ever walk on our playground?
- How can it be so cold in springtime? (This one's easy: We live in Denver!)

Ever since the day the wise woman and her secret entered the children's lives, Wonder Boxes have been spotted in the lunchroom, on the playground, at home, and on field trips. Magnifying glasses have found their way into them, as well as shiny pebbles, feathers, dead bugs, "diamonds," flower petals, and "dinosaur fossils."

And I have begun to do some wondering of my own. Since when have I looked closely at a bustling anthill and wondered what goes on underneath? Since when have I taken the time to pick up a roly-poly and watch it curl into a little ball? And since when have I tried to catch snowflakes in my coat sleeve, just to see if I'd be the first to find two the same?

Children everywhere know that the secret of wisdom is to be curious about the world, to open up their senses and see, hear, taste, touch, and smell life's treasures. Giving children time to explore their world, ask questions, and pursue those questions that matter to them most lets them know I value their curiosity outside the classroom as well as inside. My job is to continue to nurture their wonder and work to awaken my own.

Evidence of Understanding and Independence

"When you have lots of questions about a book, that's good. Then you know there's going to be a lot of learning coming to you."
Daniel

"I think that sometimes kids can learn stuff that grown-ups can't. A kid's brain isn't as stuffed with things they have to do, so they have more room to think and see and ask questions about things they don't already know the answers to."
Lilli

"When you ask questions, it makes you want to keep reading so you can figure them out. It keeps your head in the book."
Madison

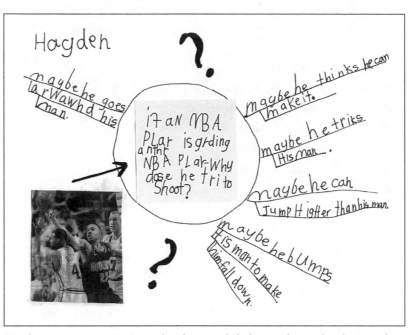

Hayden creates a questioning web at home to help him understand a photograph in the newspaper

Why do there Parents not have Wings but the baby ones do? Thinking. maybe because that's the way thay were borne or when they grow up ther wings disaper,

Madison's question about *Catwings* by Ursula LeGuin

A group exploration

Daniel's quotation about *Strega Nona* by Tomie dePaola

"Asking questions is smart. It means you don't understand something and you know *you don't understand it*."
    Bret

"Sometimes you never get the answer to your really strong questions, but you should still keep working to figure them out, because the answer can come to you another day."
    Whit

Wat is the
tailypo?

Who is saying
tailypo tailypo?

are the Blak
skrachis from the
tailypo?

wot hapined
to the old man?

If the tailypo
onlea ripet the
coveres, howcome
the hol house is gone?

Chris's questions before, during, and after reading *The Taileypo* by Paul Galdone

The Magic Fish

When I read
these Words I
dont Want togo
Siad the fishermen
go! Siad his
Wife. I'M Wondering
Why the wife Wants
So meny things?
Why dosint go
her silf? she
Shodint make the
fishermen go?
                    Bret

Bret's response to *The Magic Fish* **by Freya Littledale**

Asking Questions at a Glance

What's Key for Kids?

- Readers spontaneously and purposefully ask questions before, during, and after reading.
- Readers ask questions to
  clarify meaning
  speculate about text yet to be read
  determine an author's style, intent, content, or format
  focus attention on specific components of the text
  locate a specific answer in the text or consider rhetorical questions inspired by the text.
- Readers determine whether the answers to their questions can be found in the text or whether they will need to infer the answer from the text, their background knowledge, and/or an outside source.
- Readers understand that many of the most intriguing questions are not answered explicitly in the text, but are left to the reader's interpretation.
- Readers understand that hearing others' questions inspires new ones of their own; likewise, listening to others' answers can also inspire new thinking.
- Readers understand that the process of questioning is used in other areas of their lives, both personal and academic.
- Readers understand that asking questions deepens their comprehension.

(Adapted from Keene and PEBC)

Tried and True Texts for Asking Questions

All I See by Cynthia Rylant
Amelia's Road by Linda Jacobs Altman
An Angel for Solomon Singer by Cynthia Rylant
Fly Away Home by Eve Bunting
Grandfather Twilight by Barbara Berger
The Lotus Seed by Sherry Garland
Monarch Butterfly by Gail Gibbons
The Stranger by Chris Van Allsburg
The Trumpet of the Swan by E. B. White
Why Is the Sky Blue? by Sally Grindley
The Wise Woman and Her Secret by Eve Merriam
Yanni Rubbish by Shulamith Levey Oppenheim

Emily shares her learning with the class.

Why Do Dog's have Wet noses?

some PePPel thenk Dog's have Wet nose's To keep there nose's cool. Most of the time a happy Dog licks it's nose. When a Dog's sick it's nose is Dry.

10

Determining Importance in Nonfiction

Children determine which questions they want to pursue further.

W hen are you going to teach us about *those* kind of books?" Madi asks during share time, pointing to the red tubs of books labeled Dinosaurs, Flight, Reptiles, Biographies, Animals, Cars and Trucks, Magazines, Field Guides, First Discovery Books, Newspapers, Maps and Atlases, Big Cats, Disasters, and more.

"You mean the nonfiction?" I answer, surprised. The rest of the class is nodding, pointing, and bouncing up and down, letting me know they're interested in knowing more about those kinds of books, too. "We-ell," I say, "how about Monday?" Whoops of joy erupt from the troops, but I'm thinking, "What are you *saying*? Monday's only three days away!"

We'd been learning how and why readers determine importance in fiction, and I'd been planning to wrap things up and move on to something new. We'd spent five weeks on this strategy already, and the children had learned how readers identify key themes in stories, make predictions about the stories' organization and content, and use what they'd learned about the characteristics of fiction to distinguish important from unimportant information. And they'd learned that determining what's important in fiction often depends as much on the reader as it does on the text.

But now Madi had me thinking. I thought about her question and realized how smart of her it was to wonder about "those kind of books." I'd assumed that somehow children already knew that nonfiction books involved reading to learn—they'd been looking at and reading these books all year, hadn't they? And I'd assumed that if they could read and understand stories, they could read and understand informational books, too. I hadn't really considered the importance of explicitly teaching them the difference.

I'd have taken a day or two to teach them about the table of contents, the index, maybe even the glossary in such books—and, of course, to explain that nonfiction gives us information that is true. But Madi was after more than that. She'd learned how to determine importance in fiction. I suspected she was wondering how to go about doing that in nonfiction—and how to learn from those kinds of books, too.

That weekend I lugged home about twenty nonfiction books, vowing to make good on my word. As I read through them, I noted their distinguishing characteristics and features, determining which ones I thought were most important for children to learn. But by the time Sunday evening rolled around, it became clear that before I could teach children how to use the features of nonfiction in purposeful ways, I had to teach them what nonfiction was.

Monday morning the meeting area is a sea of books about snakes, dolphins, gemstones, sharks, kittens, puppies, wolves, the ocean, shipwrecks, the human body, flowers, space, earthquakes, astronauts, cowboys, ballerinas, dinosaurs, soccer, Tiger Woods, volcanoes, bugs, and big trucks. My purpose? Just as we teach children to use math manipulatives by giving them time to "free explore" what they are and how they work, giving them time to explore nonfiction provides them (and you) with experiences to build on when more explicit teaching begins.

The children's eyes light up when they enter the room; it's almost as if I've laid out doughnuts and milk. They scurry over, devouring one book after another. "Ooohs" and "Aaahs" and "Check this out!" and "OHMYGOSH!" and "Can I have that shark one next?" let me know my plan is a good one. Their enthusiasm is contagious—before long I'm down on the floor right along with them, ooohing and aaahing and learning myself.

Questions naturally arise, and out come the Wonder Boxes. Children begin recording questions like mad. "How can a wolf capture an elk when the elk is so much bigger?" Devon wants to know (Figure 10.1). "Why are some twisters big and others small?" Chris wonders. "How does a puppy get out of its mama's tummy?" Caroline, Nicole, and Meghan ask (Figure 10.2). "This is perfect," I think to myself. Children are loving the explo-

FIGURE 10.1 Devon's question

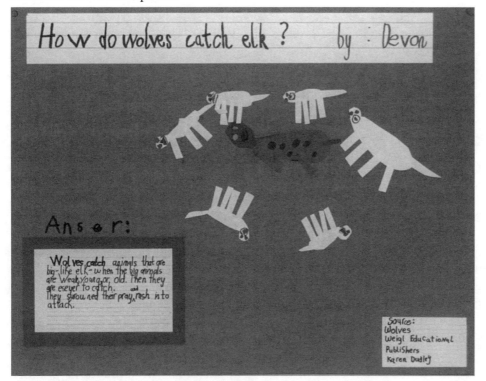

FIGURE 10.2 "How do puppies come out of their mama's tummy?"

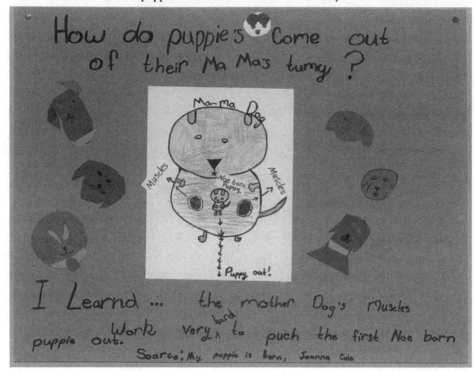

ration of nonfiction, their interest in Wonder Boxes has been renewed, and they will have a wider variety of questions to choose from when it comes time to select their most important ones and read for specific information.

Modeling Differences Between Fiction and Nonfiction

I begin by holding up a copy of *Grandfather's Journey* by Allen Say. "What type of text do you predict this is?" I ask. "Fiction!" the children reply. "Knowing that it's fiction, how might you expect the story to be organized?" Andrew predicts the story will have "a beginning, middle, and end." Others predict a setting, characters, a problem, some events that connect to the problem, and a resolution.

"Good thinking!" I tell them. "You remembered what we learned about fiction and how it is organized. Now can you predict what the story might be about?" Wyatt predicts it might be about somebody's grandpa who once went on a journey across the ocean to America. He thinks he's "probably going to have some trouble on the way, like maybe robbers or a war or something like that. But then he'll meet some nice people and make some new friends and get married and have kids and live happily ever after."

I want Wyatt and his classmates to be this confident and articulate when they make predictions about the organization and content of nonfiction text, too. Just as with narrative text, teaching children that expository text has predictable characteristics and features they can count on before they read allows them to construct meaning more easily as they read.

I hold up a book entitled *Bugs! Bugs! Bugs!* by Jennifer Dussling. "What do you notice about this type of text?" I ask the children as I leaf through the book and read parts of it aloud. "It's totally about bugs!" Cole answers. "You're right!" I tell him. "It is all about bugs. You noticed right away that this kind of text is organized differently than fiction.

"You won't find a beginning, middle, or end in books like this. And you won't find characters, problems, or resolutions either. Instead, these kinds of books—you already know them as *nonfiction*—are organized around specific topics and main ideas, and they try to teach you something. Nonfiction writing gives you information that is true. Let's read it and see what we can learn. . . ."

Another day I talk with the children about how they can use what they know about this type of text to make predictions about its content—what the text might teach them. I say, "Remember when Wyatt was able to predict what might happen in *Grandfather's Journey*? He was able to do that because he's learned, just like the rest of you, what to expect when you read fiction. When readers read nonfiction, they make predictions about the text, too. But they don't make predictions about the *kinds of things they expect will happen.* They make predictions about the *kinds of things they expect to learn.*

"When readers make predictions about what they'll learn, they activate their schema about the topic *and* what they know about the type of text they are about to read. Take a look at this book—*Nature Watch Spiders* by Barbara Taylor. Right away, because of its title and the photographs on the cover, I can tell it's a nonfiction text and it's going to be about spiders. See all the different kinds of spiders on the cover? I don't know a lot about spiders, but I do know they have eight legs, they spin intricate webs, and they're part of a group of small creatures called arachnids.

"I'm predicting this book will be about all the different kinds of spiders in the world, and that maybe I'll learn about where they live, what they eat, their life cycles, and even which ones are dangerous to humans." I flip through the book, checking the table of contents, the headings, and the index, explaining how these features help me make predictions about the text. I do the same with two or three other books.

The next day I ask the children to help me make predictions. I release responsibility by

- asking children to bring a nonfiction book they haven't read to the meeting area, get eye-to-eye and knee-to-knee with a partner, and make predictions about what they expect to learn.
- spreading fiction and nonfiction materials out in the meeting area, asking children to get a partner, choose two or three items, and ask themselves, "Is this fiction or nonfiction? How do we know?"
- asking children to bring a nonfiction book and a fiction book to the meeting area, get into pairs, and create a Venn diagram that shows the two books' differences and similarities. We then create one large diagram that combines everyone's thinking (see Figure 10.3).

In his book *I See What You Mean,* Steve Moline writes, "If we teach children that all reading is 'reading for story' we overlook many key strate-

FIGURE 10.3 Venn diagram: fiction and nonfiction

Name *All of us!*
Title *What have we come to expect when we read fiction and nonfiction?*
Venn Diagram

Fiction
- beginning, middle, and end
- setting
- characters
- problem
- events
- resolution
- pictures
- stories
- themes
- read from front to back

Title
illustrations
they help you learn
they are fun to read
words

Nonfiction
- index
- bold print
- table of contents
- photographs
- captions
- headings
- cutaways
- diagrams
- information
- ideas
- amazing facts
- read in any order

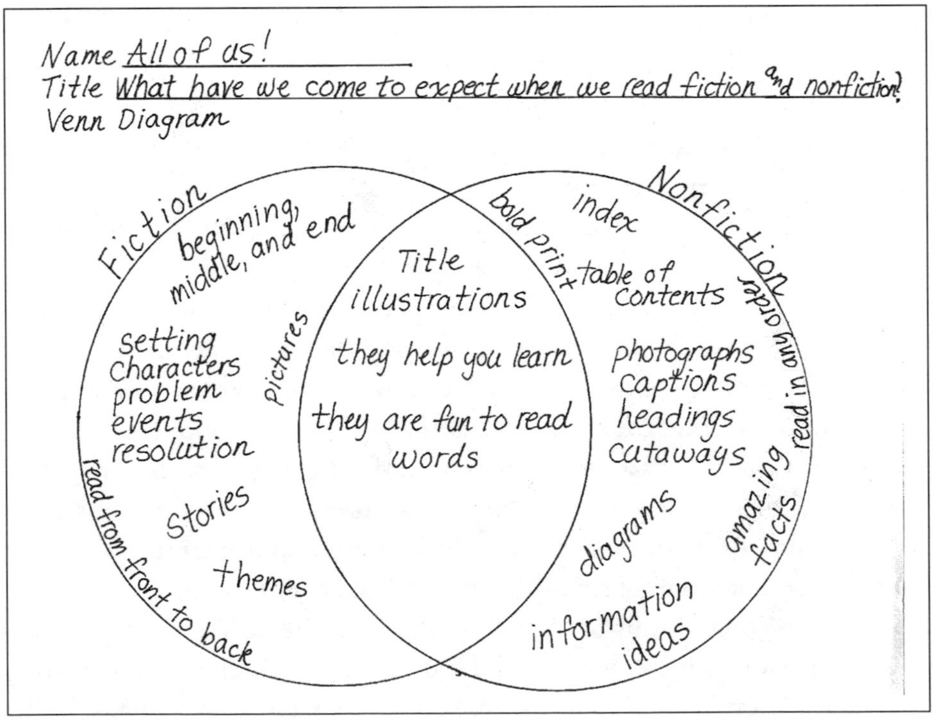

gies that we employ when reading selectively. Some of these strategies include scanning, skimming, accessing the text through the index, using headings and signposts to the information we want or just strolling through the pictures in order to orientate ourselves in the text" (p. 8).

Children are surprised to learn that depending on their purposes for reading, they don't have to read the text in order. I model using the various nonfiction strategies, showing the children what it looks like, and what my thinking is, as I skim and scan, access the index and the table of contents, use the headings to guide me, read the picture captions, and so on—all to find out what I need to know. I think aloud, too, about the information I want to remember, and show how I use sticky notes, highlighters, and my notebook to keep track of my learning.

Noticing and Remembering When We Learn Something New

"Have you ever thought about the way you respond to new information?" Steph Harvey asked me one day as we sat chatting away about nonfiction in her sunlit writing room. "Have you ever noticed what your inner voice says when you learn something new?" "Not really," I answered, understanding the inner voice part but unsure about what it was supposed to be saying. "It's something to think about," she said, "and I have a hunch it's important." (We don't always talk about this stuff, but sometimes we just can't help it.)

"Here, take a look at this," she said, handing over a well-read *National Geographic*. "Think aloud as you read, and you'll see what I mean." I open the magazine's familiar yellow-bordered cover and land on an article called "Deadlysilk" by Richard Conniff. "Wow, Steph, listen to this!" I say after a few minutes. "Did you know that some spiders eat their webs and reweave them up to five times a day? That's amazing! I never knew that! And get this—it's the female spider who does all that weaving—once the males reach maturity they wander around making love, not war. I didn't know that either!"

Steph's staring and smiling at me, for once silent. "What?" I say, throwing up my hands. "Did you hear yourself?" she asks, rattling off "Wow!" "Listen to this!" "That's amazing!" "I never knew that!" and "Get this!" adding, "See how those words signal you you're learning something new?" "Oh my goodness," I say, "you're right!" (Add "Oh my goodness" to the list, too.) We go on to yak about something else, but as usual, Steph has me thinking.

"Boys and girls," I say the next day, "wait until you hear what I learned from my friend Steph yesterday." I tell them the whole story, and think aloud some more about the spider and its remarkable web to show them what I mean. They want to discover their inner voices, too, and record the words that help them recognize they're learning something new on chart paper.

Soon I hear their cries:

"*Awesome!* Can you believe some ants squirt smelly acid when they're scared?"

"*Sweet!* It takes only eight and a half minutes for a space shuttle to reach space."

"*Cool!* Jumbo jets in the future will have two stories and can carry more than five hundred people! I never knew that!"

"*Whoa!* When Mount Vesuvius erupted it buried the city of Pompeii under a layer of ash that was twenty feet thick. That's as high as our school!"

"*Yikes!* I just learned that a meteor the size of Mount Everest hit our planet sixty-five million years ago and maybe caused the dinosaurs to be extinct!"

"So how will you remember all the things you've learned?" I ask. "I know!" Meghan volunteers. "Let's put an **N** and an **L** on a sticky note for 'new learning,' and then just write the most important part—and the title of the book, and the page number, too, so we can find it and read it again if we need to." It's unanimous.

Convention Notebooks

My teammate Michelle DuMoulin and I knew the importance of teaching our kids about the conventions, or features, of nonfiction. We knew this helped focus and support young readers, and that even emergent readers could determine importance and construct meaning by paying close attention to features such as photographs, diagrams, captions, and comparisons. But we also knew we needed to build children's background knowledge and explicitly teach them what nonfiction conventions are, what kinds of information these conventions give us, and how they help us determine what is important in a text. We knew *what* we wanted to teach kids; it was the *how* that had us stymied. We vowed, as we sometimes do, that we wouldn't go home until we had a plan.

That evening Convention Notebooks were born! We finally figured out (hunger may have had something to do with it) a way to teach kids to recognize, remember, and begin to understand the purposes of the nonfiction features they found. Measuring nine inches square, Convention Notebooks contain twelve or so sheets of blank white paper and a construction paper cover and back. This is how they work:

Each day for two weeks Michelle and I focus on a different convention. Say our focus is on comparisons. Before class, we search our nonfiction libraries for at least five or six places where comparisons have been used and flag the pages with sticky notes. When it's time for the lesson, the children and I locate and name the comparisons we've found and read the surrounding text aloud. But noticing and naming nonfiction conventions are not enough. We also think aloud about how they help us as readers; we think aloud about the purpose of each one.

Next, Michelle and I ask children to find examples of that same convention in books from the classroom or the library and either record one example in their notebooks or create an example of their own. Children share their discoveries in small groups each day, and we record our learning on a two-column anchor chart headed "What do we know about nonfiction conventions?"

Convention	Purpose
Labels	Help the reader identify a picture or photograph and/or its parts
Photographs	Help the reader understand exactly what something looks like
Captions	Help the reader better understand a picture or photograph
Comparisons	Help the reader understand the size of one thing by comparing it to the size of something familiar
Cutaways	Help the reader understand something by looking at it from the inside
Maps	Help the reader understand where things are in the world
Types of print	Help the reader by signaling, "Look at me! I'm important!"
Close-ups	Help the reader see details in something small
Tables of contents	Help the reader identify key topics in the book in the order they are presented
Index	An alphabetical list of almost everything covered in the text, with page numbers
Glossary	Helps the reader define words contained in the text

Convention Notebooks not only build background knowledge for text features that children encounter in their reading, but they also can be used as resources when children are asked to synthesize information in order to answer research questions. The notebooks help children think through which convention(s) would showcase their information best.

Locating Specific Information

Throughout our study of questioning and nonfiction, I ask the children to place a Wonder Card or two into a basket. Two or three days a week we draw one out and search for its answer. First I model for children what I do when I want to find out specific information. I show them how to think aloud about certain questions:

- What do I already know about the topic?
- What type of book or other source will help me best?
- Where will I find the information?
- How is the information organized in the source? How will I go about locating what I need?

Then, after I've looked through the source of information:

- What did I learn? How can I synthesize my learning for myself and others?

I gradually release responsibility to children by asking the same questions of the whole group. When (or if) we find the answer to our Wonder Card question, the child who asked the question records its answer on the back of the card and cites the source (author, title, date). Later I ask children to get into small groups or pairs; each group draws a question from the basket and works together to explore the answer. Questions we can't answer are posted outside the classroom, under a sign that reads "HELP! Can you help us with the answers to these questions? If you can, PLEASE write a note to us and put it on our teacher's desk. [At this point we include a map to show readers how to get to our classroom.] Thanks from all of us in Room 104."

Throughout this study I work closely with Jennifer Shouse, our talented librarian. She teaches the children about call numbers, where reference materials are located in the library and the kinds of information they provide, and how to access Ask Jeeves, the World Book Online, and *First Connections: The Golden Book Encyclopedia* on the computer. When children print out information, Jennifer and I teach them to write in the margins and highlight the key concepts they want to remember.

■ ■ ■

By now, the children have learned some of the characteristics of nonfiction. They've learned how to distinguish it from fiction, and how to make predictions about its organization and content. They've become familiar with the features of nonfiction books and their purposes, and how to locate specific information. Most important, they've learned that reading nonfiction is about reading to learn. I think they're ready to put all that learning to good use. Bring on the Wonder Boxes, and let's find out!

I ask children to find a spot in the room, spread out their Wonder Cards, and choose three or four questions that they care about most. "Which ones are you most passionate about?" I ask. "Which ones come from your heart?" Once they've decided, I ask them to put the questions they've selected in order of importance at the front of their Wonder Boxes.

They can't wait! The next day they arm themselves with their Wonder Boxes, sticky notes, bright yellow highlighters, pencils, and notebooks, and descend on the library and into the corners and spaces of the classroom, spreading their materials out on tables and floor. I'm struck by their independence. No one is asking me where the reptile books are, or to read their book to them, or wandering aimlessly about. And not one soul is copying sentence after sentence into a notebook.

Children synthesize and share their learning in a variety of ways. These decisions are essentially theirs to make. I used to show the children examples of ways to share their learning, but I've come to believe that limits their capacity to think creatively. I make sure materials are in ample supply, including posterboard for those who want it; I ask only that the children include their question, evidence of what they learned, and at least one nonfiction convention, and that they cite their source(s) of information. The next section shows some of the ways children share their learning.

Evidence of Understanding and Independence

"Bold print and headings tell you what the author thinks is important. The index and table of contents let you choose for yourself."
Wyatt

"Themes go with fiction and learning goes with nonfiction."
Maddy

"You know how when it rains? The grass and flowers and trees soak up all the water they need, and the rest just runs on down the street. We soak up what's important to us, too, and let the rest of it go away."
Christopher

"The feelings that stories leave you with let you know what's most important."
Nina

Exploring why dogs bark

Jamie's ladybug

Reading with Meaning

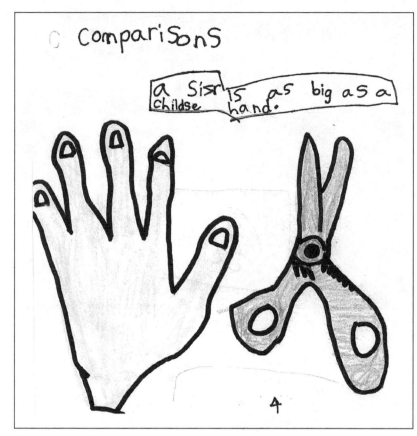

Comparisons

a Sisr is as big as a childse hand.

4

Megan's comparison

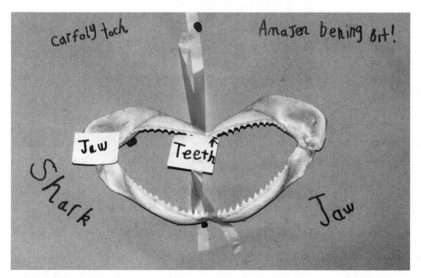

carfoly toch   Amajen bening Bit!

Jaw   Teeth

Shark   Jaw

"Imagine being bit"

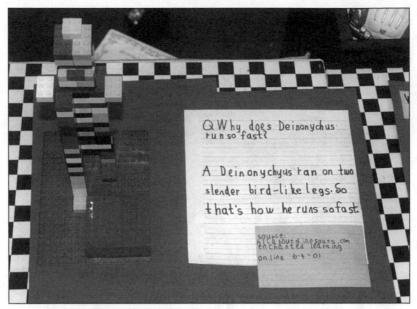

Mitch's project, "Why does deinonychus run so fast?"

School Rools
No- smocing
No- biting
No- fiting
No- liying
NO- tatoos.

Frank determines which school rules are most important

Determining Importance at a Glance

What's Key for Kids?

- Readers distinguish the differences between fiction and nonfiction.
- Readers distinguish important from unimportant information in order to identify key ideas or themes as they read.
- Readers use their knowledge of narrative and expository text features to make predictions about text organization and content.
- Readers utilize text features to help them distinguish important from unimportant information.
- Readers use their knowledge of important and relevant parts of text to answer questions and synthesize text for themselves and others.

(Adapted from Keene and PEBC)

Tried and True Texts for Determining Importance in Nonfiction

Series:
>   Dorling Kindersley Readers, DK Publishing, New York
>   I Can Read About . . ., Troll Associates, New York
>   First Discovery Books, Scholastic, New York
>   Eyewitness Books, Knopf, New York

Newspapers:
>   Your local paper
>   *Weekly Reader,* Box 120033, Stamford, CT 06912

Magazines:
>   *National Geographic for Kids,* National Geographic Society, 17th and M Sts. N.W., Washington, DC 20036
>   *Time for Kids/Big Picture Edition,* Time, Inc., Time-Life Building, 1271 Avenue of the Americas, New York, NY 10020
>   *Ranger Rick,* National Wildlife Federation, 8925 Leesburg Pike, Vienna, VA 22184
>   *Zoo Books,* Wildlife Education Ltd., 9820 Willow Creek Rd., San Diego, CA 92131
>   *Calliope: World History for Young People,* Cobblestone Publishing, 30 Grove St., Peterborough, NH 03458
>   *Kids Discover,* 170 Fifth Ave., New York, NY 10010
>   *Cobblestone: The History Magazine for Young People,* Cobblestone Publishing, 30 Grove St., Peterborough, NH 03458

Field guides:

Peterson Field Guides for Young Naturalists, including volumes on songbirds, backyard birds, caterpillars, and butterflies. Houghton Mifflin, Boston, MA.

National Audubon Society First Field Guides, including volumes on reptiles, weather, trees, shells, amphibians, fishes, rocks and minerals, insects, and the night sky. Scholastic, New York.

CDs:

First Connections: The Golden Book Encyclopedia. Western Publishing Co./Josten Learning Corp.

National Geographic Society, various titles (1-800-342-4460)

For a more complete list of resources please see the Appendixes and References in *Strategies That Work: Teaching Comprehension to Enhance Understanding* by Stephanie Harvey and Anne Goudvis. 2000. Stenhouse Publishers, Portland, ME.

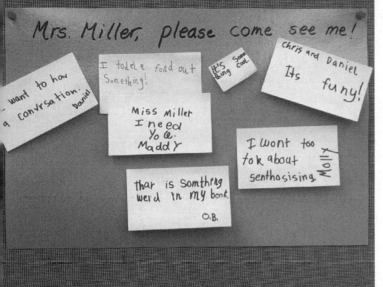

11

Synthesizing Information

Writing a note to the teacher keeps interruptions to a minimum during conferences.

Emphasizing writing in response to reading enhances comprehension.

157

F rank pushes "play" and "Oh, What a Beautiful Morning" blasts out of the CD player. Whit quickly adjusts the volume, and the class and I sing our way over to the meeting area. Frank invites us to read the morning message they've written; he points to the words as we read, "Hi, everybody! Whit and Frank are going to teach a lesson on **SYNTHESIS** [all caps, bold print, red marker] today. Are you up for a challenge?"

A chart entitled "Whit and Frank synthesizing *Oliver Button Is a Sissy*" is push-pinned to the board. Below the heading they've drawn seven 3-by-5-inch rectangles, just the size of their sticky notes, with plus signs separating each one. After the seventh one, they've drawn a big equals sign with the words "Finl Sinthasis" written after it. I'm not sure exactly what they're up to, but I can't wait to find out. I'm pretty sure it's going to be good.

It's more than good. "You know how we've been learning about synthesis?" Whit begins. "Well, Frank and I had so much thinking about it that we want to share it with you. Frank is going to read *Oliver Button Is a Sissy* aloud, and I'm going to show you how we synthesized it. Are you ready?"

Frank reads the Tomie dePaola story aloud, and on the pages containing a sticky note, on which is written their synthesis of the story so far, Whit stops the story, reads the note, and places it in one of the squares (see Figure 11.1). When they get to the equals sign, Whit says, "So you see how we got to the final synthesis? We just kept adding on and adding on and adding on to our thinking. It got bigger and bigger and bigger, and now we totally know what the book is all about! You might want to try it in your reading today. Happy reading!"

■　■　■

My colleagues and I had been studying synthesis for years. We even wrote an article about it for *Language Arts* in December 1996. But I never seemed to get very far with it in the classroom. "Oops!" I'd say. "It's the middle of May. No time for synthesis again this year." (You may guess the real reason why I never got around to it.) So what changed? What made a difference? What helped me understand that synthesis is more than just a fancy name for summary? It was Ellin Keene who asked me questions just like these one night after school.

She found me with my shoes off, sprawled on the floor, surrounded by charts and children's work. I'd spread everything out, thinking about how I might write this, the last chapter of the book you're reading, on synthesis. She kicked her shoes off, too, and joined me on the floor. We were

FIGURE 11.1 Whit and Frank's synthesis

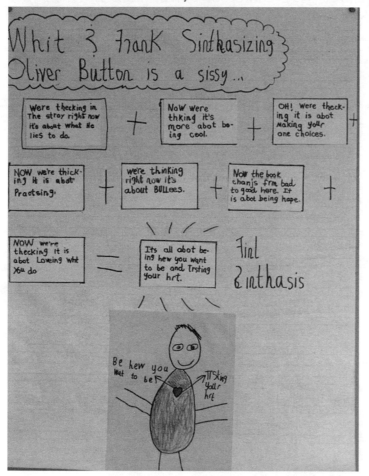

struck by the kids' work, and she asked me again: "Come on. What made the difference?"

"It's the ripple, Ellin," I answer. "Remember when we were fooling around with synthesis several years ago, and you launched it with *Tea with Milk* by Allen Say? You told me it was simple elements of thought transformed into a complex whole. But you told the kids that synthesis is like throwing a rock into a pond: first there's the splash, and then the water ripples out, making little waves that get bigger and bigger. You likened that to synthesis, remember? You said that as you read, your thinking evolves as you encounter new information, and the meaning gets bigger and bigger, just like the ripples in the pond. I kept playing with that analogy and two years later, voila!"

Ellin leaves, but I remain sprawled on the floor, still surrounded by papers, still wondering how best to share what I've learned about synthesis.

I take a look (again) at Whit's drawing of Oliver Button with the big red heart, Ben's synthesis wheel and his amazing definition, and the synthesis of *The Story of Jumping Mouse* that Max has recorded in his notebook. I decide that the children are the ones who can help me.

Anchor Lessons

Readers monitor overall meaning, important concepts, and themes as they read, understanding that their thinking evolves in the process

I explain the ripple in the pond metaphor to the kids, and read and synthesize the book *Smoky Night* for them. That afternoon I transfer my synthesis word for word (or nearly) onto a chart entitled "Synthesizing *Smoky Night* (think aloud by Mrs. Miller)" (see Figure 11.2). I want the children to be

FIGURE 11.2 Synthesizing *Smoky Night* by Eve Bunting

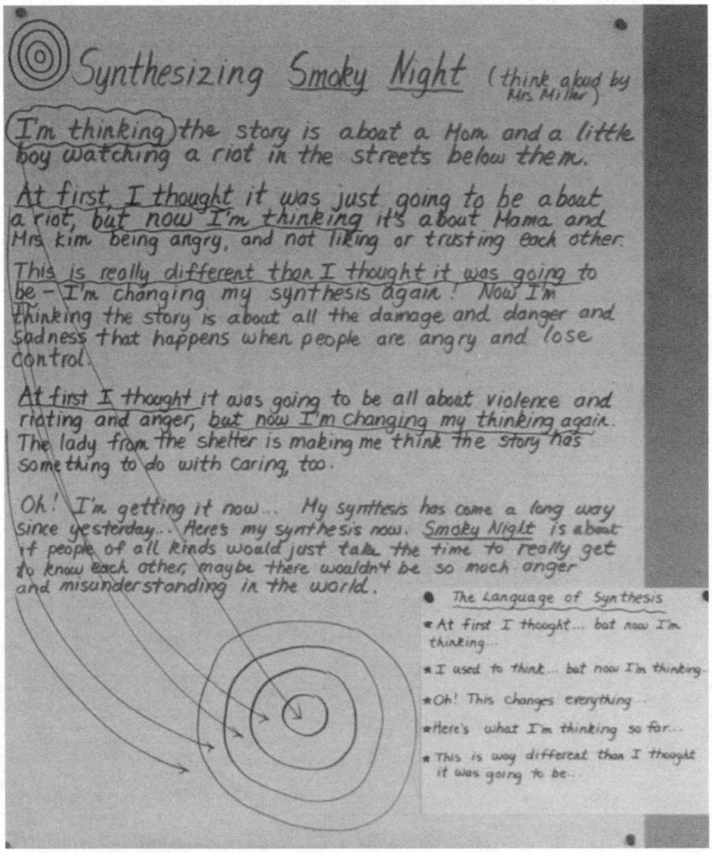

able to take a closer look at how my thinking evolved as well as help them begin to track the language of synthesis.

Children catch on quickly—it seems as though we've been building up to this moment all year—and they're eager to have at it on their own. Ben asks me to make a record sheet "that has the ripple on it," and that night I'm happy to comply. We use the sheet to record the evolution of our thinking as we read *The Alphabet Tree* by Leo Lionni, and many later opt to use it to keep track of how their thinking evolves as they read independently. (See Bret and Maggie's written synthesis of *A Color of His Own* by Leo Lionni, Figure 11.3.)

Not Ben. He pulls me to the side, thrusts the record sheet my way, and scrunches up his face. "This isn't really what I meant," he tells me, shaking his head. When I ask him "what he really meant" he says, "Here, let me show you." He draws a small circle on the back of the sheet, then another, larger one around the first; I can tell now he's going for the *full* ripple effect. "I see what you mean, Ben, but won't it be hard to write in a circle?" I ask him. "No," he answers, "it'll be *easy*!"

It was. I drew the form to his specifications and Ben tried it out the next day, requested a few minor adjustments, and was then ready to teach his classmates how it worked. It was a hit, of course, and not even one child

FIGURE 11.3 **Bret and Maggie's synthesis**

FIGURE 11.3 Bret and Maggie's synthesis

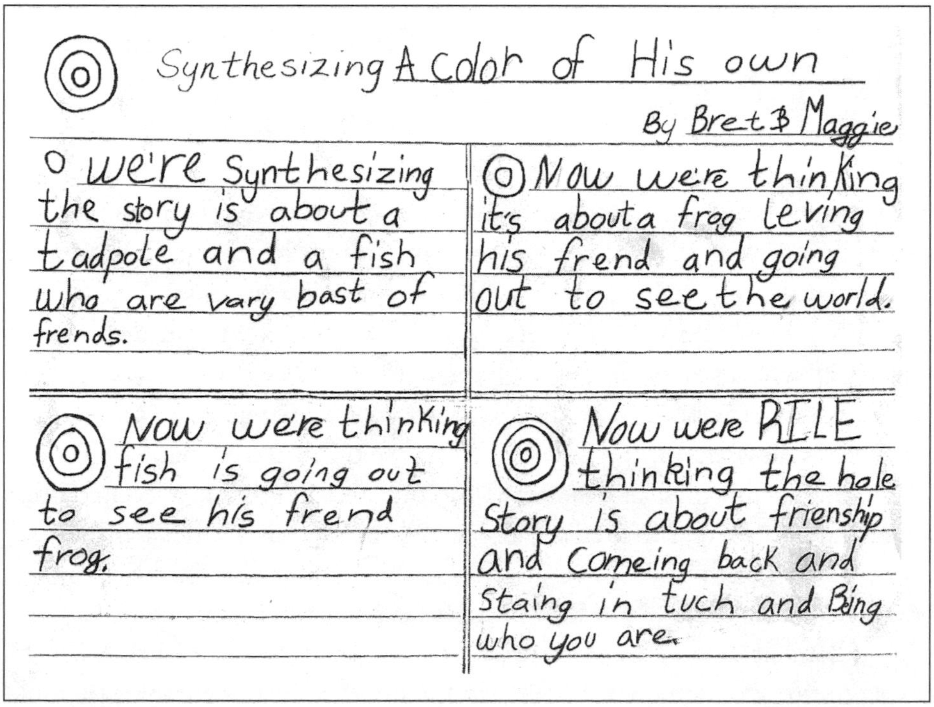

Synthesizing A Color of His own
By Bret & Maggie

◦ We're Synthesizing the story is about a tadpole and a fish who are vary bast of frends.

◎ Now we're thinking it's about a frog leving his frend and going out to see the world.

◎ Now we're thinking fish is going out to see his frend frog.

◎ Now we're RILE thinking the hole story is about frienship and comeing back and staing in tuch and Bing who you are.

FIGURE 11.4 Ben's synthesis wheel, as rendered by Rian and Madi

got dizzy. (As for their teacher? Well . . . have you ever tried reading in a circle?) Rian and Madi's synthesis of *The Library* in Figure 11.4 uses the form that will forever be known as "Ben's synthesis wheel."

"So, Ben," I ask him several days later, "now that you are such an expert at synthesizing, how would you define it? How would you explain synthesis to somebody who didn't know what it means?" He fumbles for the words he wants, and finally says, "Let me think about that."

Fifteen minutes later he seeks me out and hands me a construction paper circle. "Here, I figured it out," he tells me. "This is what synthesis is."

"It's beautiful, Ben," I say, admiring the brightly colored blue, orange, red, and green circles, "but how does this explain synthesis?"

"Let's sit down," he says, realizing this may take some time, "and I'll explain it to you. See the blue circle in the middle? That's what you're thinking first. Then see the next circle? The one that's mostly orange with just a little bit of blue? It shows how you still keep some of your beginning thinking, but when you learn more, you have even more thinking to add to it. Your thinking gets bigger. See the third circle? It's got some blue, and some orange, but it's *mostly* red, because now there's even more new thinking, you're going deeper and deeper into the text. And see the next one? It's mostly green. You see, the ripple isn't just a *solid* line; some of the best thinking leaks right on through." (See the last page of the color insert.)

I'm speechless. Ben, age six, has captured (synthesized?) the nature of synthesis. Where was he ten years ago when I needed him? (Oh, right—he wasn't even *born*.) I think his work is so brilliant I stop the entire workshop so Ben can share what he's done with his classmates. They're not nearly as impressed. "We can draw synthesis, too!" they inform me, and they can—and do. (See pages 169 and 170 for Rian and Madison's representations of synthesis.)

Readers retell what they have read as a way of synthesizing

I think of retelling as a fairly literal recounting of what children have read, learned, and remembered. To give the kids a framework for thinking about retelling as they synthesize what they've read, I teach them to

- tell what's important,
- in a way that makes sense,
- without telling too much.

When teaching children how to retell as they synthesize fiction, I model the activity using familiar picture books and fairy tales. The children already know how stories are organized; their identifying the setting, characters, problem(s), an event or two, and the problem's resolution help focus and support their understanding of the book.

When teaching kids to retell information in nonfiction text, the framework for thinking remains the same, but the focus is on what they have learned, rather than the elements of story. I show them how to take notes by writing down only a few important words—just enough to help them remember what they've learned—and ask them to share their learning, sometimes orally, sometimes in writing, in their own words.

I gradually release responsibility by

- stopping now and then as I read a story aloud, asking children to get eye-to-eye and knee-to-knee in order to synthesize the text so far, then collaborating and charting their thoughts in the whole group;

- asking children to read independently for five or ten minutes, then stopping them to find a partner and retell the story or what they have learned in their own words;
- asking children who are reading the same text to synthesize it when they finish, then get together and compare their thinking.

I've learned that some of the best ways to give children practice and highlight some of the purposes of retelling occur in the moment. For example, when Maggie comes back after being absent, I might say, "Welcome back, Maggie! We read another chapter in *My Father's Dragon* while you were gone. Would you like someone to retell it for you?" Or "We read a book about the Underground Railroad while you were gone. Who will synthesize what we learned for Maggie?"

During share time, when a child is talking about a book most of the class is unfamiliar with, I might say, "Molly, could you synthesize your book for us? That will help us better understand your point."

When a child is going on and on about a story, a movie, a sleep-over, or a play date, I might say, "That sounds so cool [or fun, or interesting]! Take a minute and see if you can synthesize all that information. Remember, think about what's important, tell it in a way that makes sense, and try hard *not to tell too much*!"

And I often say at the end of the day, "When you go home today and your mom or dad says, 'What happened in school today? What did you learn?' what might you say? Let's synthesize our learning now so you'll be ready!"

Readers capitalize on opportunities to share, recommend, and criticize books they have read

Children recommend books to each other all year long (see the photo at the start of Chapter 4), and I give them opportunities to synthesize the books they recommend. I bring in several book reviews from the newspaper, and together the children and I decide on what information to include and what form their review will take. Whit's recommendation of *Oliver Button Is a Sissy* is shown in Figure 11.5. His review does a fine job of telling what's important in a way that makes sense without telling too much.

Readers extend their synthesis of the literal meaning of a text to the inferential level

"Lilli, would you like to share your synthesis of the story?" I ask. I'd just read John Steptoe's *The Story of Jumping Mouse* aloud, having paused at cer-

FIGURE 11.5 Whit's review of *Oliver Button Is a Sissy* by Tomie dePaolo

tain points for the children to write down their thoughts on the story. "Yes, thank you," answers Lilli. (Figure 11.6 shows her writing):

> I'm thinking it is about a mouse who is going to go on an adventure to find his dream. But now I'm thinking he will get caught by the snake and he won't be able to go on his adventure.
>
> And now I'm thinking he will get to the far-off land with the help he gets from the animals, and his hope and faith. And along the way he will meet more animals to give and to get help from. Maybe it is like a heaven place and he will get his smelling back and his seeing back and all he things he lost, he will get back.
>
> And now I'm thinking he will be able to now see and hear because the magic frog turned him into an eagle and he got back what he had given away.
>
> I think the lesson is, if you give you will get more than you gave.

FIGURE 11.6 Lilli's synthesis of *The Story of Jumping Mouse* by John Steptoe

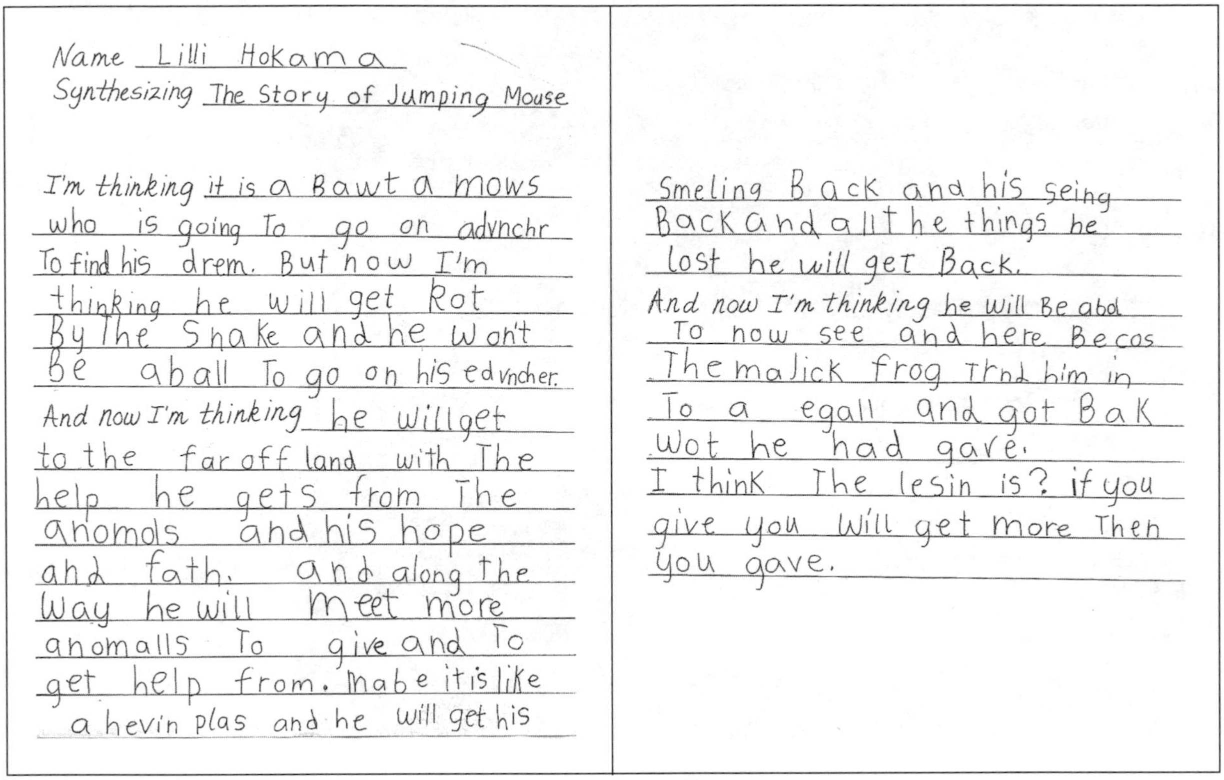

Name _Lilli Hokama_
Synthesizing _The Story of Jumping Mouse_

I'm thinking it is a Bawt a mows who is going To go on advnchr To find his drem. But now I'm thinking he will get Rot By The Snake and he won't Be aball To go on his edvncher. And now I'm thinking he will get to the far off land with The help he gets from The anomols and his hope and fath. and along the Way he will meet more anomalls To give and To get help from. mabe it is like a hevin plas and he will get his

smeling Back and his seing Back and all the things he lost he will get Back. And now I'm thinking he will Be abd To now see and here Becos The malick frog That him in To a egall and got Bak wot he had gave. I think The lesin is? if you give you will get more Then you gave.

Figure 11.7 shows Max's perspective on the same story.

For this lesson, I tell children I will read a story aloud, and that they'll be asked to synthesize both during and after the reading. I tell them it doesn't matter how they choose to synthesize, only that they do it in a thoughtful, organized way. Once children have selected the supplies they need, we regroup in the meeting area and I begin the story. I read for a while, then stop for them (and me) to synthesize the story up to that point. I repeat the procedure three or four more times, giving children time at the end to reflect and connect their thinking into a larger, more meaningful whole.

The Story of Jumping Mouse wasn't the first story we read this way. I began with fables. I'd read several familiar ones aloud and do a basic retelling for the children, thinking aloud about how I infer the lesson, or moral, of each one. Fables are great here—they're short and you can do two, three, or even four in a day, showing children how readers extend their literal synthesis (of the fable) to an inferential one (the moral or lesson).

Children love listening to fables, sitting with a partner to retell and infer their lessons, and of course just sharing them. Fables can take over work activity time, too, what with children acting them out, writing their own, and creating scenes, characters, and events from their favorites with wooden blocks, Legos, and Beanie Babies.

Once children have worked with fables for a while, I increase the sophistication of the read-alouds with stories like Lauren Mills's *The Rag Coat,* Byrd Baylor's *The Table Where Rich People Sit,* Estelle Condra's *See the Ocean,* John Steptoe's *The Story of Jumping Mouse,* and Arnold Lobel's *Fables.* It was right after the *Jumping Mouse* lesson that Whit and Frank created their *Oliver Button* chart. And as you may imagine, it wasn't long before other charts were vying for space on walls, cupboards, and doors.

As I finish this last chapter on synthesis, I'm thinking, as I always do when I finish a comprehension study, "What worked well? What didn't?" and "What might I do differently next year?" I'm also thinking about what I learned this year about synthesizing and learning from Whit, Ben, Lilli, and their twenty-four classmates. I'm struck again by their intelligence and the amazing potential they bring to the classroom.

Ben's artistic definition of synthesis helped me understand that as readers encounter new information, it doesn't necessarily change everything that has come before. Readers actively revise their synthesis as they read but "some of the best thinking leaks right on through." Lilli and Max, through their synthesis of *The Story of Jumping Mouse,* taught me that the search for meaning is different for each child because meaning is constructed from individual cognitive processes. And Whit's depiction of Oliver Button and the words, "Be who you want to be. Trust your heart" showed me that keeping a cognitive synthesis during reading can help the reader identify and depict themes that connect to the overall meaning of the text.

■ Evidence of Understanding and Independence

"Synthesis is like inferring, only super-sized!"
Madi

"If you don't ever change your mind, you're not really synthesizing."
Mitchell

"Synthesizing is like putting a puzzle together. You have to sort out your thinking and put it in the right place."
Cory

> Dear mrs. miller,
> By the Way we should get togather again. It was fun. I do Know your Background Knoledge is connected with Synthesis.
> When your new thinking comes in it Knocks over all the old thinking and the new thinking takes over. But the old thinking is not gone fore-ever. It stays there and becomes your Back-ground Knoledge, It all connects togather,
> right? Riley

Riley's summer letter, still contemplating synthesis

Reading with Meaning

> to infer is to argue with the pros and cons, with the characters, the ups, the downs, the feelings, the emotions, the life, and the time in the story. To infer is to place yourself in the place, the time, the character. To infer is to creatively mold <u>your</u> thoughts, <u>your</u> feelings, <u>your</u> background knowlege into the story.

Isabella's synthesis of inferring, as a third grader

Children's synthesis of *The Lazy Bear* by Brian Wildsmith

Rian's definition of synthesis

At fiste it is a little bit
of theking. Then biger theking
comes and you add and add
on and you take your old
theking and your new theking
and put them together.

Frank's definition of synthesis

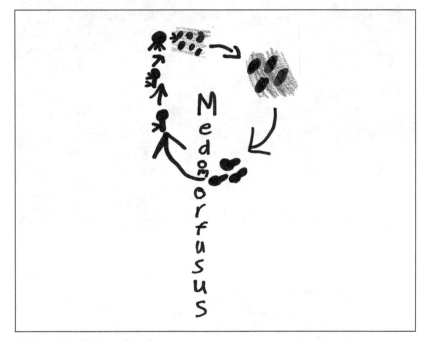

Madison's definition of synthesis

Synthesis at a Glance

What's Key for Kids?

- Readers monitor overall meaning, important concepts, and themes in text as they read, understanding that their thinking evolves in the process.
- Readers retell what they have read as a way of synthesizing.
- Readers capitalize on opportunities to share, recommend, and criticize books they have read.
- Readers extend their synthesis of the literal meaning of a text to the inferential level.
- Readers synthesize to understand more clearly what they have read.

(Adapted from Keene and PEBC)

Tried and True Texts for Synthesizing Information

The Alphabet Tree by Leo Lionni
Charlie Anderson by Barbara Abercrombie
Fables by Arnold Lobel
Frederick's Fables by Leo Lionni
Oliver Button Is a Sissy by Tomie dePaola
The Rag Coat by Lauren Mills
See the Ocean by Estelle Condra
Smoky Night by Eve Bunting
The Story of Jumping Mouse by John Steptoe
The Table Where Rich People Sit by Byrd Baylor
Tea with Milk by Allen Say

Epilogue: In June

It's a late afternoon in June. The children have gone, and save for a lone cricket (could it possibly be the same one?) chirping from the bug box in a faraway corner, the room is quiet. It's the last day of school, and my desk is a heap of bath beads and oils, plates of candy and cookies, a pair of purple dangling earrings, roses, daisies, plants, and gift certificates for movies, a facial, and—glory be!—a ninety-minute massage.

But I know what lies underneath all the goodies. There are the cumulative records into which I need to glue children's pictures and record test scores, a ratty-looking register I must reconcile and ink in, and report cards I have to mail to those children who are already on summer vacation. And then there's the room that needs to be packed up, the plants that need to be wedged into my trunk for their yearly pilgrimage to their summer home, and piles of thank-you notes that need to be written and mailed.

What's a teacher to do? This one makes her way over to the once-white chair in the corner and settles in to watch the sunlight as it streams in through the windows. I think about my animal lovers, Irish step dancers, and Kenny Loggins enthusiasts. I wonder what life will hold for them, and I wish for a peaceful world that appreciates all they have to offer.

Gone are the interviews and portraits with their too-high-on-the-fore-head eyes, crinkled-paper hair, glued-on earrings, and bright red lips that once smiled back at me. Crayons and pencils, once pointed and lying just so, are but little nubs of lead and wax. Picture frames that held the smiles of this year's girls and boys are empty. And I'm feeling, as I always do this time of year, just a little empty myself.

My eye catches the dry-erase board across the way. "Dear First Graders," it reads. "Welcome to first grade! You are going to LOVE it!!! Love, the Second Graders."

Taped right below the message is a poem entitled "Like Magic."

Just when I'm about to get misty, Ellie, whom I've known since she was three, races into the room and jumps into my arms. "I'm in first grade now!" she proclaims. "And guess what? You get to be my teacher!"

Like Majic

When
I
came
to
First Grade
I
did int
know
how
to
read.
I
Just
hesutatid
and
Then
My
swch
turnd on
the
light
and
then in
a Flash
I learnd how to read, it was Butuful, like Majic.

References

Children's Literature

Abercrombie, Barbara. 1990. *Charlie Anderson.* New York: M. K. McElderry Books.

Adoff, Arnold. 2000. *Touch the Poem.* New York: Blue Sky Press.

Aliki. 1975. *The Two of Them.* New York: Mulberry Books.

Altman, Linda Jacobs. 1993. *Amelia's Road.* New York: Lee & Low Books.

Arnold, Tedd. 1987. *No Jumping on the Bed.* New York: Penguin.

Atwater, Richard, and Florence Atwater. 1938. *Mr. Popper's Penguins.* Boston: Little, Brown.

Avi. 1995. *Poppy.* New York: Orchard Books.

———. 1998. *Poppy and Rye.* New York: Avon Books.

Barchas, Sarah. 1975. *I Was Walking Down the Road.* New York: Scholastic.

Baylor, Byrd. 1994. *The Table Where Rich People Sit.* New York: Macmillan.

Bentley, Dawn. 1998. *The Three Little Pigs.* Kansas City, MO: Piggy Toes Press.

Berger, Barbara. 1984. *Grandfather Twilight.* New York: Philomel Books.

———. 1997. *A Lot of Otters.* New York: Penguin Putnam.

Brinkloe, Julie. 1986. *Fireflies.* Chicago: Scott Foresman.

Brothers Grimm. (Retold by Barbara Cooney.) 1965. *Snow White and Rose Red.* New York: Delacorte Press.

Brown, Marc Tolon. 1985. *Hand Rhymes.* New York: E. P. Dutton.

Brutschy, Jennifer. 1993. *Winter Fox.* New York: Knopf.

Bunting, Eve. 1988. *How Many Days to America? A Thanksgiving Story.* New York: Clarion Books.

———. 1991. *Fly Away Home.* New York: Clarion Books.

———. 1994. *Smoky Night.* San Diego: Harcourt Brace.

———. 2001. *The Wall.* New York: Clarion Books.

Carlstrom, Nancy White. 1987. *Wild, Wild Sunflower Child.* New York: Macmillan.

———. 1993. *What Does the Rain Play?* New York: Macmillan.

Coffelt, Nancy. 1993. *Dogs in Space.* San Diego: Harcourt Brace Jovanovich.

Condra, Estelle. 1994. *See the Ocean.* Nashville, TN: Ideals Children's Books.

dePaola, Tomie. 1975. *Strega Nona.* New York: Prentice Hall.

———. 1979. *Oliver Button Is a Sissy.* San Diego: Harcourt Brace Jovanovich.

———. 1988. *Now One Foot, Now the Other.* New York: Trumpet Club.

Dodd, Anne Westcott. 1992. *Footprints and Shadows.* New York: Simon & Schuster Books for Young Readers.

Donnelly, Judy. 1987. *The Titanic Lost and Found.* New York: Random House.

———. 1988. *Tut's Mummy Lost and Found.* New York: Random House.

Downs, Robert Bingham. 1964. *The Bear Went over the Mountain.* New York: Macmillan.

Dussling, Jennifer. 1998. *Bugs! Bugs! Bugs!* New York: DK Publishers.

Finch, Mary. 2001. *The Three Billy Goats Gruff.* New York: Barefoot Books.

Fox, Mem. 1988. *Koala Lou.* San Diego: Harcourt Brace Jovanovich.

———. 1994. *Tough Boris.* San Diego: Harcourt Brace Jovanovich.

Francen, Mike. 1999. *I Have a Dream.* Tulsa, OK: Francen World Outreach Publications.

Gagliardi, Maria Francesca. 1969. *The Magic Fish.* New York: Putnam.

Galdone, Paul. 1977. *The Taileypo.* Boston: Houghton Mifflin.

Gannet, Ruth Stiles. 1997. [1948]. *My Father's Dragon.* New York: Random House.

———. 1987. My Father the Dragon Series. New York: Random House.

Garland, Sherry. 1993. *The Lotus Seed.* San Diego: Harcourt Brace Jovanovich.

Gibbons, Gail. 1989. *Monarch Butterfly.* New York: Holiday House.

Greenfield, Eloise. 1978. *Honey, I Love, and Other Love Poems.* New York: Crowell.

Grindley, Sally. 1997. *Why Is the Sky Blue?* New York: Simon & Schuster Books for Young Readers.

Hansel and Gretel. England: Ladybird.

Harris, Beth Coombe. 1993. *Little Green Frog.* Lewisville, TX: School of Tomorrow.

Heard, Georgia. 1992. *Creatures of Earth, Sea, and Sky.* Honesdale, PA: Wordsong.

Henkes, Kevin. 1991. *Chrysanthemum.* New York: Greenwillow Books.

Hill, Barbara Tinker. 1976. *The Little Yellow Duck.* [n.p.]

Hoffman, Mary. 1991. *Amazing Grace.* New York: Dial Books for Young Readers.

Houston, Gloria. 1992. *My Great-Aunt Arizona.* New York: HarperCollins.

Howard, Jane R. 1985. *When I'm Sleepy.* New York: Dutton.

Keats, Ezra Jack. 1996. *The Snowy Day.* New York: Viking Press.

Kilborne, Sarah S. 1994. *Peach and Blue.* New York: Knopf.

Kramer, S. A. 1997. *Ice Stars.* New York: Grosset and Dunlap.

Kraus, Robert. 1970. *Whose Mouse Are You?* New York: Aladdin Books.

———. 1986. *Where Are You Going, Little Mouse?* New York: Greenwillow Books.

Langstaff, John M. 1974. *Oh, a Hunting We Will Go.* New York: Atheneum.

LeGuin, Ursula. 1988. *Catwings.* New York: Orchard Books.

Lewis, C. S. 2000. *The Lion, the Witch, and the Wardrobe.* New York: HarperCollins.

Levy, David H., ed. 1996. *Stars and Planets.* New York: Time-Life Books.

Lindgren, Astrid. 1950. *Pippi Longstocking.* Trans. by Florence Lamborn. New York: Viking Press.

Lionni, Leo. 1968. *The Alphabet Tree.* New York: Pantheon.

———. 1975. *A Color of His Own.* New York: Pantheon Books.

———. 1985. *Frederick's Fables: A Leo Lionni Treasury of Favorite Stories.* New York: Pantheon Books.

Littledale, Freya. 1966. *The Magic Fish.* New York: Scholastic.

Lobel, Arnold. 1972. *Mouse Tales.* New York: Harper & Row.

———. 1977. *Mouse Soup.* New York: Harper & Row.

———. 1980. *Fables.* New York: HarperTrophy.

Long, Sylvia. 2000. *Hush Little Baby.* San Francisco: Chronicle Books.

Marshak, Suzanna. 1991. *I Am the Ocean.* New York: Arcade Publishers.

Martin, Bill, Jr., and John Archambault. 1989. *Chika Chika Boom Boom.* New York: Simon & Schuster Books for Young Readers.

Marzollo, Jean. 1978. *Close Your Eyes.* New York: Dial Press.

Mayer, Mercer. 1977. *Just Me and My Dad.* Racine, WI: Western.

Mazer, Anne. 1991. *The Salamander Room.* New York: Knopf.

McLerran, Alice. 1992. *Roxaboxen.* New York: Puffin Books.

McKissack, Patricia. 1986. *Flossie and the Fox.* New York: Dial Books for Young Readers.

McKissack, Patricia, and Frederick McKissack. 1944. *The Little Yellow Duck.* Danbury, CT: Children's Press.

Mellonie, Bryan, and Robert Ingpen. 1983. *Lifetimes: A Beautiful Way to Explain Death to Children.* New York: Bantam Books.

Merriam, Eve. 1992. *Goodnight to Annie: An Alphabet Lullaby.* New York: Hyperion Books for Children.

———. 1993. *Quiet, Please.* New York: Simon & Schuster Books for Young Readers.

———. 1999. *The Wise Woman and Her Secret.* New York: Aladdin Picture Books.

Mills, Lauren. 1991. *The Rag Coat.* Boston: Little, Brown.

Milton, Joyce. 1992. *Wild, Wild Wolves.* New York: Random House.

Minarik, Else Holmelund. 1957. *Little Bear.* New York: Harper and Row.

Mountain Streams: Nature's Relaxing Sounds. 1999. Sounds of Nature. Masters Series. Compact disc.

Munsch, Robert N. 1980. *The Paper Bag Princess.* Toronto: Annick Press.

Muse, Clarence. 1932. *Way Down South.* Hollywood, CA: D. G. Fischer.

My First Real Mother Goose Board Book. 2000. New York: Scholastic.

Opie, Iona, ed. 1999. *Here Comes Mother Goose.* Cambridge, MA: Candlewick.

Oppenheim, Shulamith Levey. 1999. *Yanni Rubbish.* Honesdale, PA: Boyds Mills Press.

Park, Frances, and Ginger Park. 2000. *The Royal Bee.* Honesdale, PA: Boyds Mills Press.

Parish, Peggy. 1985. *Amelia Bedelia Goes Camping.* New York: Morrow.

Penn, Audrey. 1993. *The Kissing Hand.* Washington, DC: Child Welfare League of America.

Raffi. 1989. *Five Little Ducks.* Illus. by Jose Aruego and Ariane Dewey. New York: Crown.

Robinson, Martha. 1995. *The Zoo at Night.* New York: Margaret K. McElderry Books.

Rosen, Michael. 1990. *Little Rabbit Foo Foo.* New York: Simon & Schuster Books for Young Readers.

Rylant, Cynthia. 1983. *Miss Maggie.* New York: Dutton.

———. 1985. *The Relatives Came.* New York: Bradbury Press.

———. 1988. *All I See.* New York: Orchard Books.

———. 1991. *Night in the Country.* New York: Macmillan.

———. 1992. *An Angel for Solomon Singer.* New York: Orchard Books.

Saunders, Dave, and Julie Saunders. 1990. *Dibble and Dabble.* New York: Bradbury Press.

Say, Allen. 1993. *Grandfather's Journey.* Boston: Houghton Mifflin.

———. 1999. *Tea with Milk.* Boston: Houghton Mifflin.

Sendak, Maurice. 1962. *Chicken Soup with Rice: A Book of Months.* Nutshell Library. New York: HarperCollins.

———. 1963. *Where the Wild Things Are.* New York: Harper & Row.

Seuss, Dr. 1963. *Dr. Seuss's ABC's.* New York: Beginner Books.

Shaw, Charles Green. 1947. *It Looked Like Spilt Milk.* New York: Harper.

Squire, Ann. 2002. *Gemstones.* New York: Children's Press.

Steptoe, John. 1972. *The Story of Jumping Mouse: A Native American Legend.* New York: Lothrop, Lee & Shepard.

Stewart, Sarah. 1995. *The Library.* New York: HarperCollins.

Stock, Catherine. 1993. *Where Are You Going, Manyoni?* New York: Morrow Junior Books.

Stoltz, Mary. 1993. *Say Something.* New York: HarperCollins.

Taylor, Barbara. 1999. *Nature Watch Spiders.* New York: Lorenz Books.

Thomas, Shelley Moore. 1995. *Putting the World to Sleep.* Boston: Houghton Mifflin.

Van Allsburg, Chris. 1986. *The Stranger.* Boston: Houghton Mifflin.

Waber, Bernard. 1972. *Ira Sleeps Over.* Boston: Houghton Mifflin.

Wang, Mary Lewis. 1989. *The Ant and the Dove: An Aesop Tale Retold.* Chicago: Children's Press.

Ward, Cindy. 1988. *Cookie's Week.* New York: Putnam.

Wells, Rosemary. 1981. *Timothy Goes to School.* New York: Dial Books for Young Readers.

———. 1985. *Hazel's Amazing Mother.* New York: Dial Books for Young Readers.

———. 1994. *Night Sounds, Morning Colors.* New York: Dial Books for Young Readers.

Westcott, Nadine Bernard. 1998. *The Lady with the Alligator Purse.* Boston: Little, Brown.

White, E. B. 1970. *The Trumpet of the Swan.* New York: Harper & Row.

———. 1999. *Stuart Little.* New York: HarperTrophy.

Wildsmith, Brian. 1973. *The Lazy Bear.* Oxford: Oxford University Press.

Wood, Audrey. 1984. *The Napping House.* San Diego: Harcourt Brace Jovanovich.

———. 1992. *Twenty-Four Robbers.* England: Childs Play International.

———. 2001. *Heckedy Peg.* Saint Paul: Minnesota Humanities Commission.

Wyeth, Sharon Dennis. 1998. *Something Beautiful.* New York: Doubleday Books for Young Readers.

Yolen, Jane. 1991. *Greyling.* New York: Philomel Books.

———. 1981. *Sleeping Ugly.* New York: Coward, McCann & Geoghegan.

———. 1996. *Mother Earth, Father Sky.* Honesdale, PA: Wordsong/Boyds Mills Press.

———. 2000. *Color Me a Rhyme.* Honesdale, PA: Wordsong/Boyds Mills Press.

Zolotow, Charlotte. 1972. *William's Doll.* New York: Harper & Row.

———. 1980. *If You Listen.* New York: Harper & Row.

———. 1984. *I Know a Lady.* New York: Puffin Books.

Professional Literature

Anderson, R. C., and P. D. Pearson. 1984. "A Schema-Theoretic View of Basic Processes in Reading." In *Handbook of Reading Research,* ed. P. D. Pearson. White Plains, NY: Longman.

Block, Cathy, and Michael Pressley, eds. 2002. *Comprehension Instruction: Research-Based Practices.* New York: Guilford Press.

Brown, A. L., J. D. Day, and E. S. Jones. 1983. "The Development of Plans for Summarizing Texts." *Child Development* 54: 968–979.

Calkins, Lucy. 1983. *Lessons from a Child.* Portsmouth, NH: Heinemann.

Duffy, G., L. Roehler, and G. Herrmann. 1988. "Modeling Mental Processes Helps Poor Readers Become Strategic Readers." *Reading Teacher* 41: 762–767.

Fielding, Linda, and P. David Pearson. 1994. "Reading Comprehension: What Works?" *Educational Leadership* 51, 5: 62–67.

Hansen, Jane. 1981. "The Effects of Inference Training and Practice on Young Children's Reading Comprehension." *Reading Research Quarterly* 16: 391–417.

Harvey, Stephanie, and Anne Goudvis. 2000. *Strategies That Work: Teaching Comprehension to Enhance Understanding.* Portland, ME: Stenhouse.

Heard, Georgia. 1989. *For the Good of the Earth and Sun.* Portsmouth, NH: Heinemann.

Keene, Ellin, and Susan Zimmermann. 1997. *Mosaic of Thought: Teaching Comprehension in a Reader's Workshop.* Portsmouth, NH: Heinemann.

Moline, Steve. 1995. *I See What You Mean: Children at Work with Visual Information.* Portland, ME: Stenhouse.

Palinscar, A. M., and A. L. Brown. 1984. "Reciprocal Teaching of Comprehension Fostering and Monitoring Activities." *Italics Cognition and Instruction* 1: 117–175.

Pearson, P. David, and M. C. Gallagher. 1983. "The Instruction of Reading Comprehension." *Contemporary Educational Psychology* 8: 317–344.

Pearson, P. David, J. A. Dole, G. G. Duffy, and L. R. Roehler. 1992. "Developing Expertise in Reading Comprehension: What Should Be Taught and How Should It Be Taught?" In *What Research Has to Say to the Teacher of Reading* 2d ed., ed. J. Farstup and S. J. Samuels. Newark, DE: International Reading Association.

Perkins, David. 1993. "Creating a Culture of Thinking." *Educational Leadership* 51, 3: 98–99.

Pressley, G. M. 1976. "Mental Imagery Helps Eight-Year-Olds Remember What They Read." *Journal of Educational Psychology* 68: 355–359.

Raphael, T. E. 1984. "Teaching Learners About Sources of Information for Answering Questions." *Journal of Reading* 27: 303–311.

Index

visual images
    creating from text, 8

Waber, Bernard, 62, 72
Wall, The (Bunting), 54
Ward, Cindy, 21
Way Down South, 36
Weaver, Connie, xii, 2
webs
    questioning, 123, 131, 132, 136
    responding through, 100
Weekly Reader, 155
Wells, Rosemary, 60, 72, 77, 92
Westcott, Nadine Bernard, 46
What Does the Rain Play? (Carlstrom), 92
When I Am Sleepy (Howard), 92
Where Are You Going, Manyoni? (Stock),
    103, 107–9, 121
Where the Wild Things Are (Sendak), 97
White, E. B., 28, 86, 140
Whose Mouse Are You? (Kraus), 20–21
Why Is the Sky Blue? (Grindley), 140
Wild, Wild Sunflower Child (Carlstrom),
    92
Wild, Wild Wolves (Milton), 21, 98
Wildsmith, Brian, 169
William's Doll (Zolotow), 98
Winter Fox (Stock), 121
Wise Woman and Her Secret, The
    (Merriam), 135, 140
Wonder Boxes, 134–35, 143–44, 151
Wonder Cards, 134–35
    for locating specific information, 150
wondering
    in personal lives, 135
    understanding through, 124–25

Wood, Audrey, 34, 80, 92
word identification, 49–52
    dramatic responses and, 82
word meanings
    determining, using schema, 108–9
    dramatic interpretation of, 111–13
    inferring, 107–9
    inferring with sticky notes, 109, 110
words
    explicit instruction about, 50–53
    mental images created from, 80–81
    signaling learning, 147–48
    sound-symbol relationships, 51
    text-to-self connections about, 61
work activity time, 103–4
working definitions, of reading strategies,
    12
worksheets, 98
World Book Online, 151
Worth, Valerie, 74
writers' workshop, 22
writing, about mental images, 84–86
writing table, 2
Wyeth, Sharon Dennis, 116, 121

Yanni Rubbish (Oppenheim), 140
Yolen, Jane, 74, 83, 92, 98, 121

Zimmermann, Susan, 2
Zolotow, Charlotte, 69, 72, 98, 116, 121
Zoo at Night, The (Robinson), 82, 92
Zoo Books, 155